ADVANCED /
VOLUME

MW00812706

HOW TO READ
THE
AKASHIC
RECORDS

MOVING DEEPER INTO THE RECORDS
ADVANCED DYNAMICS, BENEFITS
& TECHNIQUES
WITH

BILL FOSS

THE AKASHIC RECORDS CENTER
INSTITUTE FOR HIGHER LEARNING

I

Acknowledgements:

I would like to thank everyone who has contributed to the workshops and classes their time, resources and personal support during the past years of teaching abroad and during the production and constant vigilance in writing, publishing and producing these books. Also to all the practitioners, teachers and holy masters who have changed the world for the better with their presence, service and teachings and have made a personal impact on my life and the lives of countless others with continued inspiration for creativity, service, and healing.

Note: The information and exercises contained within this book are not intended to replace psychological counselling or medical attention. If you feel the need for help, contact a qualified service professional in the appropriate field. Do not attempt to engage in the meditation, visualization, or energy exercises in this book while operating tools, heavy machinery or a motor vehicle.

WHITE
WIZARD

P U B L I S H I N G

GLOSSARY

Dedication

May this Book Serve You

In Your Search for

Greater Understanding

as You Look Into

Dreams, Visions and Intuitions.

With Eyes that can See

and Ears that can Hear,

For You, the Reader,

And to All the

Workshop Sponsors & Participants

the World Over, Thanks for Helping to Make

This Book a Reality,

I Hope It Serves You Well, Enjoy!

ADVANCED ACCESS
VOLUME 3

HOW TO READ
THE
AKASHIC
RECORDS

MOVING DEEPER INTO THE RECORDS
ADVANCED DYNAMICS, BENEFITS
& TECHNIQUES
WITH

BILL FOSS

THE AKASHIC RECORDS CENTER
INSTITUTE FOR HIGHER LEARNING

VI

INTRODUCTION

*I*n these current times we seek more and more to realize or to know ourselves more quickly and with more clarity. We truly have everything we need from ancient times if we can just stop, look and listen. As we go through our lives we learn what works and also what doesn't. Often it inspires us to get on the road to health, healing and self discovery. As we do the work many of us are guided to become guides, healers and practitioners for others so that we may share what we've learned and help them move more into their selves and into the Light.

All of the knowledge and wisdom we have available to us from ancient times throughout the ages all the way to current times is extensive. Even so we still flounder as a race much of the time. While the individual and collective egos tend to wallow with life, thought and emotions, we hold ourselves back through fear and separation. We have modern marketing and advertising to thank for targeting the primal part of human consciousness. This has brought even more separation in ways of labelling everything and everyone in society. And in spite of all that it's still the creativity of humanity at work.

With all of this in play it has guided more and more people into the ideas and notions that their must be better ways to live. So many of us are guided into exploring the Great Beyond and as part of that many of us are either guided or eventually find our way to the Akashic Records. New and traditional ways of working with energy. And so many of us find our ways into working with the Akashic Records as well as many other modalities of healing and intuitive work. We are in a new phase of society where wholesome food, supplements and information to help us live a better life are more readily available.

That said, I truly feel that there needs to be even more of us doing the healing work to help ourselves and others make the shift in order to make the Great Shift that has already begun. It can and should be a more inspirational journey than a cumbersome one.

Studying the Akashic Records on this level will have the ability to bring you into alignment with your Soul energy and when this happens you are learning, clearing, healing and shifting on multiple levels which we'll talk about within this volume.

There are varying levels at which you may use this material. You may use it forthright and straight away to become an Akashic Records reader and practitioner. You may use it as experiential and evidential learning on your path to inner knowing, cultivating wisdom or just as a past time. Whatever the case may be at the very least you may have those 'meeting at the cross roads moments' in life with your own path or someone else's and you will have studied an advanced level of accessing knowledge and creative insight in a way that may truly help you to move through a life changing event more clearly. Or to help someone else through theirs.

The amazing perimeters of the Akashic Records are so vast in all of their collections of material and so creatively and readily accessed as needed to build your very own case study. A continuing interactive study of your past lives, including distant lives among the stars. A case history of your incarnations and those of your family members.

As you continue to hone your abilities to access the Akasha, you will have the possibilities to go into Earth's history or that of the collective consciousness. Either by direct intention or by osmosis of retrieving other information.

As we delve deeper into the material you will come to understand the depth of knowledge available in this volume as you read over the Table of Contents.

Volume 3 Advanced Entry contains the master key level elements that many of us want to achieve right out of the gate. Some of us are even having some of these advanced level intuitive or visionary experiences occur naturally or by surprise. Whatever the case may be, starting with Volume 1 and then moving through Volume 2 will be a direct set up into utilizing the knowledge and wisdom contained within these two books and then moving directly into Volume 3.

Enjoy yourself as you move through these creative exercises, and messages. As you continue on this journey you are embarking on a lifelong mission to change your life spiritually through the study of the intuitive mind and the Soul. This will continually unfold for you in natural and metaphysical ways throughout your life both continually and immediately.

So welcome to my world! The world of the Akashic Records and the world of your own Self Knowing, Enlightenment and Healing! You will be forever changed in your ways of perceiving yourself, others and the world in subtle to dramatic ways and all points in between.

With this I wish you the very best experiences in every way along your Soul's journey, your life's path and your Spiritual studies.

Namaste & Many Blessings.

Bill Foss 7/28/19

HOW TO READ THE AKASHIC RECORDS

MOVING DEEPER INTO THE RECORDS
ADVANCED DYNAMICS, BENEFITS & TECHNIQUES

WITH

BILL FOSS

THE AKASHIC RECORDS CENTER
INSTITUTE FOR HIGHER LEARNING

DIVINE INTELLIGENCE IS THE NATURAL COSMIC MESSAGING OF THE UNIVERSE, OF CREATOR GOD AND OF THE AKASHIC RECORDS.

Chapter 1

DIVINE INTELLIGENCE & THE AKASHIC RECORDS

From ancient times we have always looked to the heavens. Searching for our origins. Searching for our Creator. In a natural progression of coming from beyond and witnessing the great glories of nature's presence all around us through history, the mind of man began to think creatively as he looked to the stars. Up into the heavens we gazed at the celestial bodies until we gave them names and looked into great pools of water to reflect and map the stars and eventually to even build looking glasses and telescopes to be closer to the stars.

We have always wanted to be closer to God. We have looked into the great beyond in wonderment.

Could it be that we new inside on some silent level that we came from the stars? This has always been the great quest of humanity. To search for our origin. To understand 'Why we are here' and to ask 'Where are we going?' as we move forward in time.

As we look through the ages we see the ancient Vikings honoring the Norse gods and using the Runes to connect into a very natural version of Earth's Records by divining information from the symbols.

In another time and place we see the Greeks and their creative philosophical society. As they honored and communicated with the Oracle of Delphi as the Oracle spoke with energy and messages from deep within the Earth.

We find the shamans of Peru and the monumental Machu Pichu. As they lived in very high altitudes and communicated with the spirits from the heavens and nature.

As we look through the myst of time we find the old Celtic world of ancient Europe where the druids and the great sorcerers and wizards worked with earth energy and cosmic energy as they practiced looking into visions to perceive their future, distant lands and to work with the magic of nature.

As we now travel to the ancient Americas we see the meso-american tribes of Incan, Mayan, Aztec as they built step pyramids to be closer to the gods. To perform ritual for the seasons and for all things in life as they celebrated the physical world and the unseen.

The Egyptians are most noted for their connections to the stars and their knowledge of the 'gods' travelling from afar to interact with this planet. Great murals of art and statues were built to celebrate these visitors as well as the rest of their culture. The high priests were known for reading the stars and communicating with the cosmic beings as well as creating great libraries of Records deep within the Earth as they also channelled information from the Akasha. This was a precautionary measure as a result of having survived the deluge and collapse of Atlantis. They also developed great power sources to be charged by cosmic and solar energy.

In India the great holy men called siddhas studied, practiced and worked with adepts to develop sacred archives of the directories of the family trees of humanity from the Akasha and continued to archive writing it all down on collections of papyrus leaves.

As humanity looked to the stars through the seers, wizards, priests and shamans of the world, they sought information about the future and the weather patterns, neighbouring tribes and their true origins. Throughout all cultures we began to develop different ways of divining information from beyond about our origins and destiny.

The Akasha was held sacred by many cultures. It was usually connected into by secret groups and orders. Priests and high level seers. The work was usually done in mainly in private and a peaceful or quiet setting. In some areas of the world in history including medieval Europe, visionary or mystical practices were illegal by church law. Really no one else really wanted to take it upon themselves to be doing this highly sensitive work so it was often hidden away behind closed doors for that simple reason. As much as it was also considered a sacred practice and coveted by many in places of power.

Through the ages the study of the Akasha or 'sky library' was held sacred, important and even special. So those that studied the Records were usually of a certain ilk. Good natured, spiritually driven, moderately in touch with wisdom and a purpose in life often born of service whether to community, spiritually or both.

In times of separation upon the Earth the Akasha usually would show itself to those known to be of virtue and to those who would come together to practice the art of projecting into the Records. From history through to modern times The Akashic Records was deemed a special practice and those who worked with it were even protective of it's nature and existence, more out of reverence than anything else and a notion that the world just wouldn't understand.

In modern day decades from the perspective of my reawakening, the Akashic Records has more of a place within the arenas of spirituality and metaphysics than ever before on the planet. People all over the world are waking up and discovering the Records and the sacred importance of self knowing. It has been interesting to watch modern world society really spring into action in positive ways over the last decades.

As we move forward and start to become more aware of ourselves, the world around us, our planet and our origins within the Universe we start to harness or bring into play more and more the **Divine Intelligence** of life and of our Source. The Universal Intelligence.

We may also refer to this as cosmic energy, chi, prana, the Tao or the Mind of God. Divine Intelligence supersedes all things and yet is all things. The same has been said of the Tao. We can most creatively get in touch with the Divine Intelligence. When we're working through our own life path or spirituality. Maybe we're manifesting a greater version of life's reality for ourselves.

As we start to focus on the concept of Divine Intelligence working through our prayers and through our affirmations and projections as we may start to conceptualize the nature of this God-like energy. As you think about even the words Divine Intelligence there is a special vibration to them.

As we look to the Akasha we most certainly see and feel the presence of this Intelligence. The

Akashic Records holds within it the essence of Divine Intelligence that we experience in spiritual nature. This vibrational information is held within the Records and connected to us through our Soul. The Divine Intelligence of the Akashic Records echoes the higher levels of consciousness and awareness that other civilizations among the stars have already achieved, attained and some always have been at these higher levels of existence.

The secret key to evolution of our race is in learning to connect with our own Soul Records. As we experience Self Knowing one person at a time en mass, we are not only coming alive within our own experience, we are influencing everyone in our immediate family through our DNA. We are influencing and interacting with everyone one else in our Soul Group. As our own Soul lights up it gives light to the other 11 Souls of your individual 12 Soul group. You are also influencing and healing your ancestry, your blood line and your family tree. Last but not least you are influencing everyone that you come in contact with.

Divine Intelligence is the natural cosmic messaging of the Universe, of Creator God and of the Akashic Records. It interacts with all life on all levels all of the time. It communicates with us directly through others and the events of our lives, and it communicates at a cellular and even sub-atomic level.

It is our birth right to receive, interact with and utilize this Divine Intelligence in our everyday lives. The Divine knows how to take care of it's own and you are part of it's family. As you start to access the Akasha and find your way into the great Hall of Records you will feel the vibrations of the Divine. Soft and flowing, celestial and stellar. All of the nuances that you feel with your Soul when you get in touch with it. The magnificent quietude that reverberates within your Soul is calling from Creator God Source Light of All Existence as an echo or a fingerprint of that Light. Your Soul is a direct emanation of that Light.

So accessing the Akashic Records is key in bringing you one giant step closer to the nature of your true origin. Always connected and never separate, though expressing through this reality as individualized creative light beings. Our Souls await the integration of the Heart, Mind and Body through Divine Intelligence and the Akashic Records.

AS YOU GO INTO THE LIGHT CONNECT WITH
THE BEINGS THAT YOU KNOW OR FEEL THAT
WANT THE BEST FOR YOU AND ARE PRESENT IN
DIVINE SERVICE TO YOU.

Chapter 2

RECEIVING MESSAGES FROM THE LIGHT

*T*he Light emanating from the Divine Source of Creation out across the Seven Super Universes comes to us through this Universe as creation itself. It also reaches us as the conscious awareness of our Creator. The Light may represent many different things or perspectives in the moments when we are working with others to access greater levels of healing or messages. From beyond and yet through time and space the Light reaches us in every moment.

The more we connect to it and become continuously aware of it, the more it can communicate with us. Much like the vibration of cosmic prana in our atmosphere or circulating through our bodies which will act and respond in the same way. **Prana** which is the cosmic life force energy attaching itself to oxygen molecules as it enters in through the atmosphere from the stars as pure starlight energy. Prana enters into the body via the breath and supports out bodies continually both day and at night when it will replenish our reservoir of life force energy.

As we continue studying and learning all of the dynamics and terminology of metaphysics, we can become more aware of the different levels of energy as well as the different dimensions and beings on the other side through practice and study.

We are truly multidimensional beings and as we learn about everything on the other side and how we interact and participate with it, we can sometimes assume one thing for another or even pay less attention to where the connections are coming from as long as we have a connection.

Now there is something to be said for over thinking things, though, the more people pay less attention to how they are getting their information from the beyond, rather than being particular about bringing it through in a clear, concise and reverent way, the more they have the possibility of getting sorted levels of info and maybe even from sorted sources.

We need to truly stop, look and listen rather than being an open portal for anything, everything or everyone who want to come through with messages or expressions from the other side. Many of these people and beings are still working on their own journey's healing. It is fine to get a perspective view about them as long as your not becoming an open channel for them. Some people like to feel a charge of energy no matter where it's coming from. And this is one thing that often times darker energy likes to give to someone whom they feel they might be able to attract a long standing relationship with.

In ways the Light works in much the same way. The Light and the higher beings that reside within it connect naturally with people incarnate here in human form who naturally have a clear vibration. Maybe they have moved through any and all karma from other lives or even had the same higher frequency preferences in other lifetimes. The Light and the dark are both trying to recruit folks to interact with, team players if you will. When in truth everything is being guided by the Light and the Source of Creator.

Practice connecting directly into the Light. If you practice connecting into the other side of the veil this is a very big place with many dimensions and realities. As you go into the Light connect with the beings that you know or feel that want the best for you and are present in Divine service to you.

As people transition to the other side they move through the lower worlds and into the Light. Some people willingly stay on the astral or 5th dimension in order to continue to be a guide for family, friends and others who are still here in 3D reality. Often we hear of near death stories in which people tell of going into the Light and feeling immense levels of love. Often reporting that they didn't want to come back or had to stop and think about it because the vibrations there were so soothing, loving and perfect.

The Light itself is comprised of pure Love. The Light is Love. The Light emanates out from the First Moment and The Source Light of Creator. The Great Central Sun between all Universes and realities. As we connect into the Great Central Sun which we will do in an exercise, you will get to see, feel and experience that the Central Sun itself is comprised of Beings of Light and Love. These are the beings that are sent out as Messengers of the Light. Some of these beings operate as great sentinels of Light within the dimensional realities.

A great many are sent out as pure Soul Essence of Creator God. As the Soul Energy goes out across the Universes it may sit in the stars and celestial bodies. The Souls move out across creation to influence creation itself and to experience creation as it reports back to Creator God through their connection as part of Creator God His/Her/Itself. These Souls went out to inhabit all of the other civilizations among the stars eventually finding there way here to this world.

Humanity evolved and operated with a body spirit as a representational incarnation of Soul until the Celestial Souls of Creator God started to arrive. As the Celestial Souls started to blend with humans here directly from Source and from many different regions and worlds among the stars we started to grow and develop as a race. Through times of devastation from cataclysmic events the Souls were easily able to influence humanity back onto it's feet quickly.

If you watch the movie 'Interstellar' you will see a depiction of the Great Central Sun. They call it the 'Singularity' in that movie. You will also see a depiction of the Akashic Records which is quite creatively unique.

There are many Souls from many different races among the stars that have in turn travelled here to incarnate and by doing so have influenced humanity. For many it has been an easy transition and for many also not so easy as they experience difficulty in attuning to the lower frequency of 3 Dimensional reality here on planet Earth and it's levels of gravity and atmosphere. That said it is still a beautiful planet, reality and dimension to experience.

Back to the Light. The Light itself has all natural codes for healing to help an individual return to perfection of Body, Mind & Spirit. When you practice going into the Light you will find clear and easy messages to all of your problems. All the higher beings may even be working with you to work everything out in a way that best serves you. Going into the Light can take away emotional or physical pain. It can also bring you to a place of peace, inner security and joy within yourself. Tend your self towards the Light in life and see what happens. As you move into the Light in your meditations, let the Light work with you. Both your originating source and your destiny are contained within the Light. As you practice connecting with the Light it will be clearing you and healing you. It will be easier for you now to connect into the Akashic Records as the Akashic Records is part of the Light.

Much in the same way that you would practice gratitude of forgiveness, practice going into the pure white Light and see what it has to offer you. You will find there Angels, guides, family members, God, the Ascended Masters and many other unique helpers and healers.

You may also ask for an activation of spiritual vibration which makes it easier for you to connect into the Light.

ACTIVATION MEDITATION OF DIVINE INTELLIGENCE FROM WITHIN THE LIGHT

Become relaxed as you sit or lay down in a reclining position and allow yourself to continue now to become fully peaceful. Breathing in and out with long slow soft and gentle breaths. Maybe you are listening to some very soft inspiring music or tones or maybe there is silence. As you continue to allow yourself to relax you may at this time request a blue star of higher Soul vibration to be placed in your fields in front of your heart. You may also ask to have this same blue star of the Higher Soul be placed in your fields over your Forehead.

Focus on the Blue starlight as lifting your vibration as a being of Light. This blue star will clear you naturally, quickly and continually. Focus on feeling your vibration and energy being lifted. As you experience this see now a great white light overhead surrounded by blue.

As you continue to relax, focus on this white light and gently allow yourself to move up into it. As you move into the Light allow it to wash over you and fill you up. As you lay peacefully silent you may receive pictures or visions of how the Light and it's beings interact with you. Guiding, Healing, Clearing and Communicating.

Getting you in a calm and inspired state for your life's journey forward. You may remain aware as you calmly experience the interactions or you may go deep within a dreamlike state where many things happen beyond the conscious mind. Just relax and receive and know that you are well safe and protected as you stay within the Light. When you are ready come back down gently into your body and take some time to slowly reintegrate. You may want to sit quietly for a few moments and check in with yourself. How do you feel now in Body, Mind & Spirit? You may want to journal or make notes so you remember your journeys into the Light and the messages given.

Blessings to You and your Divine Activations within the Light.

MOMENT TO MOMENT WE TRAVEL THROUGH TIME
CONTINUING FORWARD OBSERVING, CREATING AND
INTERACTING WITH THE WORLD AROUND US AND
OTHERS HAVING A SIMILAR EXPERIENCE.

Chapter 3
TIME TRAVEL
USING THE
AKASHIC
RECORDS

*W*hen we think of time travel it may jog memories of science fiction movies which cater to our imagination. We will utilize these aspects as we move into the concept of time travel and use it for the purposes of self development.

If you think about we are all natural time travellers. We travel through time in this physical world in this physical body. Moment to moment we continue forward observing, creating and interacting with the world around us and others having a similar experience.

Over the course of history there were many ways of measuring time including the hour glass and the sun dial. As our culture continued to apply it's creativity and work ethic we devised ways of measuring lengths of time in order to meter our lives and multiple numbers of different events happening simultaneously. You can imagine that in ancient history for a society to be measuring the length of multiple events and their interactions with the events, this would be a great achievement of progress.

As our world became busier and busier we developed calendars to meter our days, years and seasons. The latest calendar which we use internationally now on planet Earth is the Gregorian calendar brought about in 1582 after many other versions were created and implemented over the centuries. Over the course of time there was a long period of acceptance to this calendar by different parts of the world as each country participated out of the necessity for making trade, communication and travel easier.

As we look into the Akashic Records and our own Book of Life we are usually looking from three reference points: Past, Present and Future. So we tend to be working either directly or indirectly with the vehicle of time. We are also dealing with these events in time as they relate to our location within **Spacial Reality**.

As we look into the Past for instance we find ourselves experiencing certain moments within our surroundings. This completes the movie and gives our vision a sense of time, place, reasoning, emotional connections, mental location in relation to all other surrounding moments and times.

It has been theorized that each moment is it's own reality and each thought is it's own universe. So as the mind experiences it's mental references of past, present and future we create worlds within worlds on the mental plane of existence, the 4th Dimension. Some of these thought worlds are translated into the 3rd Dimension, our current known reality and some are translated into the 5th Dimension. Some thought projections are even translated into alternate or parallel realities. As we continue forward in time and space on our journey and we become aware of all of this, we may want to create healing and clearing around certain mental patterns that we've experienced especially if they have produced undesirable results for us, our surroundings or others.

Clearing our connections to our past helps to stop the dynamic of time looping through the mind and emotions which creates our reality over and over in the same way. Time looping is a version of being trapped in time. It can seem like a mental or time-space reality prison for anyone who wakes up to what is going on within their lives through their continual life patterns and feels helpless to move past it or escape. Being aware of the box is fundamental to being able to move, think and feel outside the box.

Someone at this level who has started to wake will go through a phase of time where they are usually aware now of what happened to them and how it has affected there life while trying to sort out or apply healing to the events. All the while the mental and emotional wounds can run deep. Wouldn't it be nice if we could work through the patterns that are creating the looping effect in a quicker manner to get different results in life.

This is where we can apply the application of time travel in a visionary and spiritual way in order to affect our current life realities forward from the next moments. We can do this for childhood traumas, emotional and relationships that need healing as well as mental patterns and physical injuries.

As we access the Akashic Records we are already naturally working with the dynamics of time travel. As we connect to our Book of Life on a Soul level we first strengthen our connection by learning to relax comfortably and let go of all preconceived notions and then we start to review our personal history through the Records.

As we review our Records we are looking into preceding moments in this life and pictures, visions, events and circumstances of our other lives. We may also even look at the time spent out of physical body in between lives here. This points to *past* moments. So we are looking into the past for the purposes of observing, understanding, healing and closure. To Know the Self.

When we observe the Self in relation to past and we make peace with it we are also accepting or embracing our Whole Self at a more complete level. This brings, freedom, forgiveness and gratitude for being able to release and accept at the same time and gratitude and inspiration for going through the process. It can be a very freeing experience and in many cases life changing whether at subtle or monumental levels.

As we are experiencing the past through these guided moments of spiritual observation I now pose the question: Is this really the past? If a person has been time looping through the effects of a past situation in their life they may not be able to quickly or clearly perceive an answer to the question. Beyond this in the greater scheme of things linear time is somewhat of an illusion. It's illusionary for two reasons:

A. Linear time is a construct that we have created for scheduling our lives, society and existence.
B. Even without linear time on a moment to moment basis all that really exists is contained within the Eternal Now Moment including all past moments.

It would be that much easier to stay in a natural present moment reference point for all us without the constructs of linear time.

As we access the Akashic Records and our Book of Life there in by way of our connection to it through the Soul we are stepping into the Eternal Now on the other side and in the higher dimensions. While we are in the Eternal Now we can more easily look at past, present and future moments. If we are truly willing to release our stress, tension, anxieties and conflicts on all levels or as much as possible we can have a clear look at what we've been through, achieved and experienced in other time lines.

So as we go into the Records we are side stepping linear time and slipping into the Eternal Now where we are able to access all moments simultaneously. This is actually what your Soul is able to do on the other side of the veil undetected most of the time as it operates beyond time and space as a multi-dimensional being.

When we go into a deep state of meditation we are accessing the Eternal Now Moment. When we are sleeping we are accessing it as well.

So you may observe the Soul's dynamics as you are accessing your past lives within the Akashic Records. You are creatively doing this through a time travel portal of the conscious awareness by way of the Soul connected into the Records. With this connection stream and the Soul being enjoined to the physical body we are able to access through the mind, the senses and the body. We are able to live stream natural moments as organic data and bring it back with us where we can process, journal and ultimately come to a fuller state of knowing who we are in relation to who we have been.

Time is relative as Einstein and other great minds

have discovered. It is continual and more so elastic to the individual who is perceiving it. It ebbs and flows or speeds up and slows down. In this way many great masters of India and other lands have learned to slow down the aging process in the body and live a longer life. Some have even been able to stop time or travel beyond time on the other side to accomplish things such as manifesting and healing.

For two different people experiencing the same event, moment, or time period from their own perspectives, time can move more quickly for one person and more slowly for another based on what's going on within them and their connections to perceiving and processing the external world. This point can be helpful in your viewing into the Records as time space reality will be shifting for you as you enter in and then return.

Some people whether clairvoyant or psychic have been able to see into the future. This is interesting because the life of each individual is being written as they go from one moment to the next. It has been said that prophecies are given so that they do no have to happen. This is an interesting statement because almost always when groups of people hear a prophecy the larger part of the group usually goes there in their minds whether they admit it or not. The next time you are given information which may seem daunting think about this statement: Prophecies are given so that they do no have to happen. Maybe we don't have to take the bait meaning maybe we do not focus on a certain possible outcome therefore creating it.

There are some events that people have agreed to place into their journey prior to incarnating. The key to this is their response to these events which brings knowledge and wisdom. So if someone is looking into the future and they are seeing or feeling something coming which brings concern, that person may start doing spiritual work for clearing of any and all karma related to the event. Here's an example:

Several years ago I was in Austin, Texas preparing for an expo in Laughlin, Nevada and I saw a car wreck or something happening to the car on the way to that location. I immediately and calmly started praying for protection and clearing around that event. I also used clearing mantras on the way to the show.

As I drove into the valley along the quickly descending and very windy highway I saw why there was concern. It was a dangerous road and you really had to be alert. There were also many drivers taking the curves much faster than the speed limit. As I drove cautiously and mindfully ahead I kept that intuitive future vision in my mind and worked with it. I was clearing and healing around any auto accident possibilities.

Nothing happened until the day I was leaving.

I was in a large parking lot and there was fierce wind. As a lady pulled into a vacant space on my passenger side wearing blue blocker sun glasses, she opened her car door and the wind immediately flung the door open, and it became wedged against my door. The result was a minor scrape. The lady, by the way, fully present to the situation, exclaimed when I approached her "I didn't do that".

Actually she was right, the wind did! I just smiled on the inside and walked away knowing that I had intervened with the event creating a much lesser outcome by focusing spiritual healing and clearing energy towards a potentially dangerous future event.

The observation in all of this was that the event still happened in this reality but the effects had been changed. I had intervened with spiritual work, prayers, protection and karma clearing work which in turn changed the outcome as I was present to it. So events can be changed and not everything in the future is set in stone. Many people change there lives and diets when they are given test results or possibilities of advanced illness in their future. They may start studying spiritually or put effort into changing their outlook and responses to life and in doing so they may have the opportunity to change the karma of any impending illness.

As for people seeing the event of the future so many visions and prophecies that I have been told about many which were dated or time sensitive just never have happened. Now when someone does read into changes in the future, this may be through a connection to the group mind or group consciousness of humanity. They may be connecting with trends that the group level needs or intends to experience beyond the individual ideals of what people experience in their own paths.

Starting to become more consciously aware of time and space may give you a better outlook on your inner world and a clearer response to the world around you. In the same way if you have been overly concerned with the external then you may want to loosen up the reigns a little bit and learn to live more in the moment or even the Eternal Now Moment.

As we've been discussing moving back through time through entering into the Records, the next exercise is a version of time travel for the purpose of mental, physical and emotional healing. Enjoy.

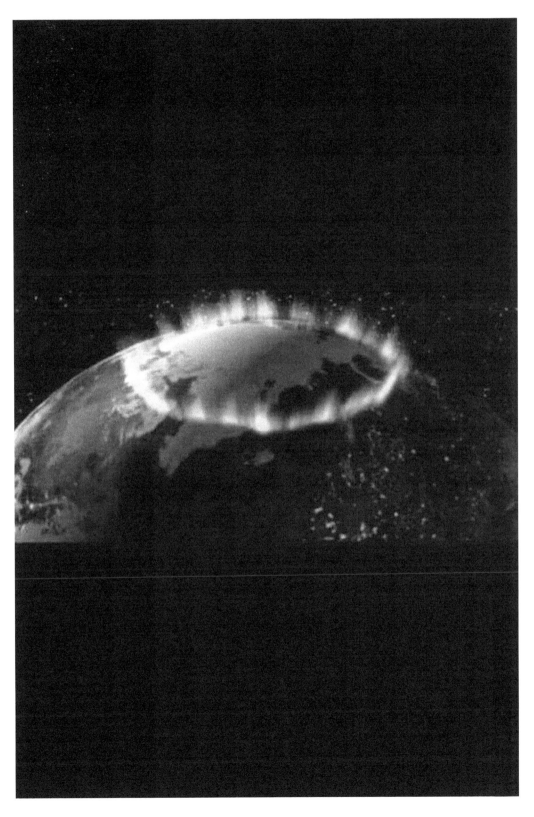

MOMENT TO MOMENT WE CONTINUE FORWARD OBSERVING, CREATING AND INTERACTING WITH THE WORLD AROUND US AND OTHERS HAVING A SIMILAR EXPERIENCE.

Exercise 1

TIME TRAVEL HEALING TECHNIQUE

*A*s you prepare to do the inner work just get into a comfortable position whether lying down or sitting in a reclined and relaxed position. Always have a glass of water within reach and a soft comfortable pillow and / or a blanket to help the body feel safe and to relax.

As you start to get comfortable and relax, really let yourself go slipping into a deeper state of relaxation. Taking some long slow deep breaths, this is your time to receive from Spirit and to interact on a deeper level for the purposes of healing. As you continue relaxing down, down , down even deeper picture a great field or sphere of gold above you. This is your Soul field. as you breath now breath your Soul field down into your body grounding your Soul within your physical body. As you merge with your Soul field you can start to feel a deep comfort coming over you as your true Self comes in and starts to take over and inhabit the physical body. Letting your ego know that your Higher Self will be taking over from here. It is no longer necessary for the ego to strain or struggle.

As you now allow the Soul to reintegrate with your physical body, see now a great portal of white light coming down and forming all around you. As this pillar of white light is becoming brighter and brighter. It starts to become so bright as it forms around you that everything else in the room and your surroundings start to become dim outside of this field. The Light is calling you up through the portal you feel yourself being drawn.

As you move up into the Light you feel it's comfort. You feel a soft and soothing feeling coming over you both physically and energetically. You are completely supported here. As we are now up in the higher dimensions of Light let's intend our selves into the Great Akashic Hall of Wisdom.

As you enter into the Great Hall you see everything very clearly through white and gold light. As we move through the Hall let's go now to the Time Travel Module which is a round room with many surrounding doorways to different times and places. As you move into the center of this room, think about something that you want to heal in your life or your past. As you think of this time or event notice a certain doorway lighting up. Looking at the door in your mind you now feel yourself moving towards it and through it as you now travel to that event in your life that you would like to support with healing energy. As you see the event coming close to you over the event horizon, you move around it and view it from all angles. You are scanning the event and yourself within it. As you move in closer you notice that everything is now moving in slow motion.

You are able to circle the event and scan it as you are now moving to the moments just slightly before it happens and you start to infuse healing energy into yourself before that time. As you bring healing energy between yourself and the surroundings your set up a healing cushion of protection that is able in this slow motion state, to start supporting you at the deepest levels.

Whatever the event is, The Akasha is showing you creatively through your mind and the Eternal Now Moment the great healing and support that you are bringing to yourself in these moments. Take your time.

As you come back from that event to the room you may think of another time and place that also could use your attention. So as you now go through one of the doorways that is lighting up and corresponding to your life event, you travel there along the event horizon and give it attention in slow motion just as you did before.

See the healing energy coming in around every part of your body in that time and space. It may even move inside of you or through you. As it also moves in between the moments of time it creates a cushion so that the time space event that you were in is supported, protected and even gently changed for the better in these moments of support.

You are very carefully changing the interaction of the event through time and space. Are you rewriting history? You may think of it in that way though in a very careful and gentle way you are intercepting any and all great levels of shock to your system in those moments, so you are in turn lessening the effects of these times and how they have impacted your total Self, your body and your life over the course of time.

You may come back to the room and go to one more event for healing. As you practice this technique you learn to control your abilities.

Coming back to the room now you enter back to the Great Hall of Light where the portal is ready to bring you back down into your physical body. As you come back into your body and your senses please take some time now to be gentle with yourself. You may want to move the body, have some water, go for a walk or write an entry in your journal about your experience.

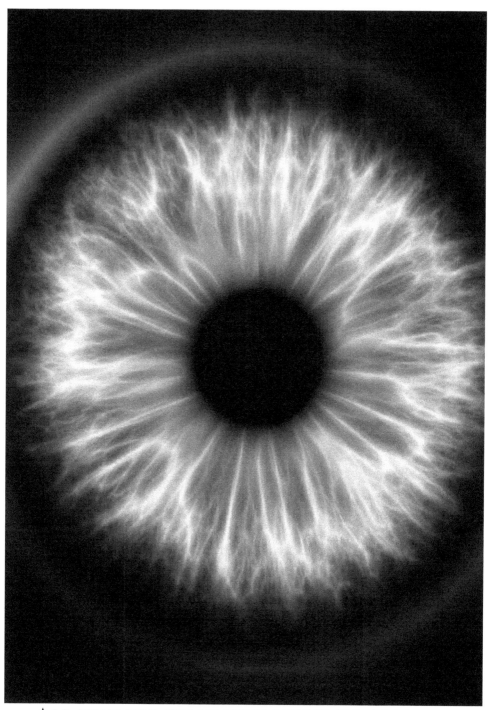

ALL THINGS THAT YOU WISH TO MANIFEST
FOR YOUR PERSONAL JOURNEY ALREADY EXIST
IN YOUR ENERGY FIELDS.

Chapter 4

HEIGHTENED LEVELS OF SEEING

*H*umanity as a culture evolving from ancient times throughout history has had many different versions of mystics as seers, wizards, sorcerers, psychics, visionaries, prophets, medicine men, shamans, medical intuitives, energy healers and the list goes on.

We may think of some of the imagery that has been used to illustrate this in our cultural storytelling such as movies, cartoon depictions or in novels. A man or a woman looking into a crystal ball as to peer either into the past, future or remotely into another location. A woman stirring a pot and looking into the liquid and seeing visions. A person looking into a stream or a still pool of water for the purpose of divining information whether from the reflection of the stars or from remote visions cast upon the water. A person looking into the ethers at visions or even astral projecting to receive information from beyond.

We have diverse and spiritually trained groups such as Buddhist monks and Hindu yogis reaching deep levels of spiritual attainment which include, astral travel, bi-location, divining information from objects in nature or reading the stars.

We might include a another spectrum akin to all of these depictions of simply tapping into the Akasha by naturally accessing the Soul energy which is directly connected to the Akasha or 'sky library.' Looking at this in similar ways is meant to give you an idea of the power of the intuitive nature of this practice. Though reading the Akasha is of a Divine nature and unique unto itself from any other type of divination. All of the other processes mentioned are either directly or subtly connected to the Akasha by way of being part of the living library we call planet Earth.

In modern times of main stream society we have labelled or categorized these things sometimes into generalities of a more superstitious nature. As we have allowed this part of our ancient history to become a distant cartoon depiction that we don't really understand, we've fallen asleep in ways that have limited our growth, foresight and evolution as a race. We truly need to leave the superstitious implications behind in order to formulate a more true to life understanding of what's actually available for us to learn about and to use it intuitively. A wide variety of metaphysical studies has often been lumped into one category making everything look as if it is of questionable origin. It's time to let go of any superstitious stories and to be able to clearly discern.

People in groups and individuals who are dabbling in magic and playing with things that they don't understand have gotten out of hand. It is creative but short sighted in desire based ritual that are usually more ego driven or based in the dark side. I'm primarily talking about novices who are attracted to the allure of supernatural television shows and such. Am I calling the kettle black?

Now if you are practicing magic and you are using your practice wisely with harm to no one and in reverent service to Earth, humanity and self, then I acknowledge your efforts.

Actually there was a lot of this happening during the dark ages as well which added to giving the practice of earth based magic a bad name. And then there were individuals who were well versed in advanced practices of both light and dark magical practices. A friend has likened practicing magic for the novice as 'a child who found daddy's gun.' I do know individuals and groups who practice with great reverence. I also know that there are individuals practicing many of the same traditions without calling it anything at all.

As we watch the movies it always seems to be the

same story: good versus evil, light versus the dark. And in order to make it more interesting the story line often has dark playing the aggressor which pushes the good right to the very point of it's own possible extinction before conquering the dark. Do we really need this over and over? Or is this a look at what might actually be occurring in the ethers or behind the scenes? The Light works smart with an all loving and all encompassing goal ultimate goal. So nothing is left unturned as it's either brought into the Light or recycled into the Light.

At some levels of the interplay between light and dark direct intervention is needed from time to time. At other times the Light and Light beings are less concerned with the dark forces as the emanations of direct Light and Love tend to drive the dark away. Dark beings and pure elemental darkness itself can be transformed into the light or it can be recycled into the Light.

When we are learning to look at light and energy how discerning are we? Can we really see what is the true Light and that which charades in the light? This is unclear for so many people. So many of us want to have an energy experience just for the sake of having an energy experience. So many more want to have the experience of gaining power or getting something from the energy experience that will build up the ego. There are many people, objects and beings practicing or operating at varied levels of vibration.

Learn to discern. Something that feels right or nonthreatening at first may prove to be otherwise once you've interacted and find out whether there is an honorable exchange of energy or not. This is a very important aspect of seeing at heightened levels.

As you continue to look in through your practice of Akashic Reading and visionary techniques you will come to a place within yourself where you start to become more overall naturally intuitive. This is when you will be more discerning with levels of vibrations around certain people, situations, objects and places. You will question things on a vibrational level more.

This is a phase that has to be gone through no matter how short or long that phase is. On the other side or future of this discerning phase, which brings you wisdom through practice, is a higher level of non-judgmental all encompassing Love, Understanding and Wisdom. This higher level still has certain levels of safety discernment through less restrictions of light and dark interactively as the duality and the oneness. At this stage you may even begin to work with and even mold the duality of reality itself through great projections of thought and emotion that are now more clear and without conflict. This is yet another level of seeing at heightened awareness levels.

As we've now covered this aspect, let's look at pure seeing itself. As your intuitive levels increase so does your psychic activity. Extra Sensory Perception and seeing into coming events. **Deja vu** or the feeling of already having had a particular experience. Clairvoyance or being able to see over a distance concerning people and events. Activating the Divine Intelligence which is universally present and using it for your intuitive arts and studies.

Sometimes your heightened awareness can be activated naturally on it's own. You may feel an energy sensation over your 3rd eye correlating with the **thalamus glad** behind the brow center in the head.

Your inner vision or Akashic vision may start to live stream without thinking about even turning it on. This may present an opportunity to just sit back and to see what you can see. Pan around a bit with your view and see if you can continue to keep it streaming without trying to control it. At times you may see something that activates or alarms the ego in some way and this can kick you out of the streaming experience. Though the more you have these types of inner visionary situations present themselves, you are chalking up more experiences of seeing. One way to trick the ego or the mind into lowering it's resistances to seeing or not seeing is this:

All experiences are a success. If you're not able to get into your visionary mind you are learning what doesn't work and this is a successful practice run. If you get in and then get kicked out by your own conflicting mental blocks or lack of focus and balance then this is also a success. A successful visionary meditation is of course also a success. You learn what works and is more effective for your practices and you also now know which approaches yielded lesser results. Whatever the case may be always be consistent in your studies and practice.

As you continue to move towards heightened levels of seeing through practice of visualizing images and situations. The practice of visualization is also synonymous with manifesting. The great blessing of synchronicity through manifesting and acquiring a more developed sense of psychic or intuitive awareness is this:

All things that you seek information on for your personal journey already exist in your energy fields. All things that you wish to manifest for your personal journey already exist in your energy fields. **Divine Timing** is the element of space time interaction that will connect you with these space time events. As you are aligning on this level you are also writing this within your own Akashic Book of Life.

Many of the things that we wish to achieve or create within our life's journey have already been placed within our energy fields and our Soul field. So many great things that you want to be part of are already part of your energy and just waiting to manifest for you! This is all part of your continual journey. In knowing this piece of information maybe there are some things that we have been focusing on that are as important for us to stop putting so much mental energy into. Our mental energy is actually very potent in conjunction with our own subconscious mind and the way these mental images hover or flow through our energy fields and into our reality. When we start to understand and to connect on this level we become more in tune with our self, our life, our world and our own power to create. In this way you are on your way to becoming a fuller more knowing being.

When you have a dream and your vision is turned on whether a fantasy movie, a symbolic message, a glimpse of the future or messages from other lifetimes and distant past, you are looking with your heightened levels of seeing and awakening. Remember to this if you think you have a block about inner seeing. Remember that you can see while you are in dreams at deeper relaxed levels and you may only need to take your ego, stress or conscious mind out of the equation in order to have a live streaming experience.

EXERCISE FOR OPENING THE INNER VISION

As you are now relaxed sitting in a comfortable position and communicate with your mind to allowing it to relax and open. As you take a few deep breaths close your eyes and just see what you see. Do you see dark black nothing? Or are there colors? Do you see images? Could you ask your mind to create an image for you? Something that you can hold in your mind and study the colors, shapes and details of? Just stay relaxed and try not to stop yourself after just starting by becoming restless or saying to yourself *'oh I just can't do it'*. Stay calm, balanced and focused. If you think you cannot do it, then simply go to any memory and look at it. Yes, instantly your inner vision is on. Remembering to someone's face or to a certain place. You may ask your mind to show you a future moment or ask a question about the future and calmly watch for an answer or symbolic message about the event. Practice this simple technique often to open your 3rd Eye.

EXERCISE 2 FOR OPENING THE INNER VISION

As you are now relaxed sitting in a comfortable position and communicate with your mind to allowing it to relax and open. As you take a few deep breaths sitting in your living space. Close your eyes and start looking very slowly at all of the things in your room. You may take a moment to study the room and it's contents in detail before you start the exercise or you may just go for it to see what details you can instantly recall about the room you are sitting in.

As you close your eyes and you visualize the room in front of you, take a moment to recognize and mentally study all of the details, shapes, colors, windows, objects, including the ceiling floors and windows. As you witness it all withing your inner vision, see if you can very slowly shift your mental view in a clockwise (right) view panning around the room. Take your time and move slowly, you can always go back and look at something you may have missed for a moment.

As you continue in a full circling pan of the room just allow yourself to see in whatever levels of shape a color feel right for you. Most people will be able to recall what's in their immediate living space just from having been around it continually. When you complete the full circle inner visionary look at your surroundings just open your eyes and see how accurate you were.

You may practice this also by holding an object in your hand or a picture. Maybe it's something in the room with a lot of detail such as a painting or detailed decorative object. As you study it closely in every way looking directly at it, now close your eyes and look at it with your inner vision. Notice the detail and shape, the color and size is still there. See how long you can hold this image in your mind as you are studying it. Then come back to the room, opening your eyes when you've completed the exercise.

Let's talk about now the two most advanced levels of seeing in relation to my teaching of the Akashic Records material here in these books that I would like to see you move towards and ultimately achieve.

The 1st is your **Live Streaming Akashic Vision**. The ultimate goal is to be able to go into the Records and to see in high definition. As you continue to practice you will have dreams, glimpses, visions or images that may be momentary or may go on for a while. As this continues at some point a deeper more vivid level of seeing may occur. This is when you are connected from your Soul into the Records. As I describe the elements surrounding this level of seeing to you, it will hopefully bring an idea of what to look for or aspire to.

One thing is for sure, when it happens you will definitely know that you've tapped into what we are talking about. This is the most vivid level of seeing that you probably will have experienced. As you look into the streaming vision, the vividly rich tones of colors will seem to be alive as they create the movies around you in your mind. So alive that it will actually be streaming energy to you as you are looking into it. This is when you truly know your Soul is connected into the Akashic Records or your Book of Life. You may have already had a meditative vision that played itself for you at such a rich level of definition. If not then keep practicing because it will surely come given the right levels of balance and relaxation in finely tuning your vision.

The 2nd is an ancient level of creative and lucid dreaming. In the ancient tribes of Africa the tribes taught each other through training the children to lucid dream. Lucid dreaming is the experience of awakening yourself during a dream sequence and participating in a way as if you were in the waking state in the 'real world.' If you've ever had a dream such as this you know how amazingly vivid it can be. The ancients taught there young not only to lucidly participate in the dream but also to control it. In the events of having lucid dreams you may have had some hair raising moments of not knowing what was going to happen next.

I believe this is why they taught there young to always be in control of their dreams. It stands to reason, if it is your vision and your dream that you are tapping into through your senses then being able to shift and control things within the dream world gives you strength and power in first person as well as clarity and skill.

So practice this before you go to sleep at night. Close your eyes and connect with your subconscious mind and tell yourself to remember your dreams. Next tell mind to wake yourself up within the dreams. And then tell your mind that as you awaken you have full control in the dreams. This gives you the power over anything that would be looming or even coming into your dream state to try and exert power over you.

Both of these processes are of a master level of seeing and will give to you insight from within yourself far beyond that which you can get from another person through messages.

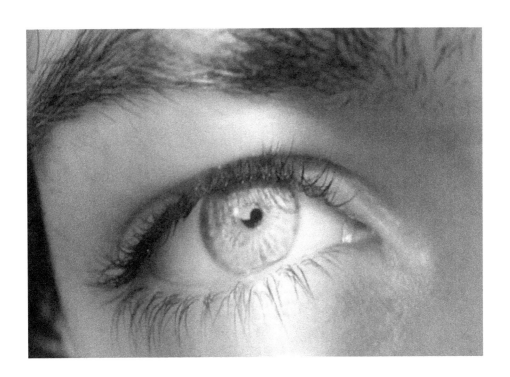

At some point You may come to understand through your visual and empathic experiences that the Akashic Hall and your Book of Life are made of living essence.

Chapter 5

MESSAGES
FROM THE
RECORDS
MADE
MANIFEST

*A*s we continue our studies of the Akashic Records we have three main time references as platforms for entry into the Records. Past, Present and Future. As we learn to hone our skills at entering to the Records and retrieving information from our past lives we are re-remembering and yet seeing some of our own hidden aspects for the first time. Some of our aspects through tendencies and habits from other lifetimes we will know quite well. the hidden or more obscure aspects are the parts that can really make an impact on our self observation and knowledge.

We may also see and discover current time reflections which give to us a truer look in the mirror as well as an expanded look at ourselves and what's really going on. Realizing yourself as all that you are is one of the most gratifying or self empowering references that you can have. This can give to us a true and even sometimes sobering look at our own life and the reality which we have made for ourselves. The ultimate look into your own self and world as 'the watcher on the hill' as the ancient teachers called it.

The next observational reference point is looking into the future and future events. This is a great point of interest with the work, to be able to see into the future. As you are in the Akashic Records and your Book of Life, there are levels of information that are given to inspire your future path. There are other informative messages that may show of a coming event that could be life altering in some way.

If this event is not a pleasurable experience the possibility of the emotions and thoughts around it could start drawing it to you. When the ego reacts to messages on this level it can also kick you out of the Akashic Live Streaming that you were using to look at the event. The best approach is to start taking preventative steps to change your life path movie in such a way as to greatly diminish the event or to even avoid it all together. By looking at future events we sometimes naturally are changing the possible outcomes of these events. Future events can have multiple possible outcomes because in our present moment reference of perceiving future events, they haven't happened yet. So there can be variations along a theme. This can be based on the thoughts we think, the emotions we charge with those thoughts and most assuredly by the actions we take between now present and then future.

Often times these events are connected to karmas or life lessons that we are meant to experience in order to get an understanding from them. So there are some that are changeable and some that may not be changeable. An interesting aspect of human awareness is to be able to endure whatever the individual is going through in the moment.

So when you see a possibility of looming events coming in the future don't let it get to you. These are usually possibilities of future 'now' moments and not set in stone. So stay in this moment and dedicate your life to being the very best you can be in this moment continually. By doing this your chances are great for changing the outcome of the event.

Looking into the past and the future have their helpful aspects for self knowing and change. That said the most powerful human perspective is always going to be 'right here and right now' or 'living in the now moment.' You may have heard expressions such as 'the now moment is all we really have'. This is fundamentally true. In any moment whether past, present or future that moment is all you had, have or will have at any point in time.

As you stay focused in the here and now you are

grounding mentally, physically and spiritually. You are also creating within the moment. Aside from your conscious inquiries into the Akashic Records, when you are connected more naturally to the here and now moment, you as more connected naturally into your Book of Life in the Hall of Records and naturally creating a more colorfully vivid life for your self interactively.

When we spend to much time lost in past events or overly concerned about future events it somewhat short circuits our present time moments and we may start looping through variations of old scenarios or becoming lost in 'what ifs' of the future. Now if you are solid on what you want to manifest for your future and you know what you are doing then that's another case and continue.

As you continue your practice of going into the Akashic Records you will be consciously having an interactive experience. At some point you may come to understand through your visual and empathic experiences that the Akashic Hall and your Book of Life are made of living essence. As you come into contact with this it will give to you a unique understanding about the way that things are made manifest from the Records.

As you are streaming you may see things appear that give you messages. As you are in the Records you may see or feel the dynamic that the pictures, objects, movies and symbols are coming from the

Records and interacting with you. You may also have the thoughts and/or feelings that these ideas are coming straight from you as you watch how they are streaming from/to both you and the Records simultaneously.

When you come to realize this you are touching into the magic of manifestation on a Soul level. What you see in the Records interacting with you has the power to play out in your 'real world events'. Even more so when you become aware of it on this level.

There are two ways in which Akashic messages can play out for you. The messages can be both literal and figurative. When I was first receiving messages from the Akashic Records there were messages that were coming through in worded messages which made me ask the question: 'Is this literal or is this figurative?'

After receiving such messages there was only one way that I could proceed,which was forward and let the messages play out in my life. In this way I could look at the original delivery of the messages in comparison to how it played out. I found that uniquely enough sometimes it was more literal and sometimes more figurative but both translations of the message were true. This really caught my attention.

This dynamic pointed to a living essence that was interacting with me from behind the scenes as well as directly and openly in life. So as you start to get messages from your own Book of Life and you start to interpret them. You may be asking yourself 'Is this a literal or is this a figurative message?' My best advice would be to wait a minute. Think about it for a while without jumping to immediate conclusions. That might be easier said than done as once something is seen or heard the mind starts to immediately consider or process the possible outcomes.

If you are intending to take actions in your life based upon a message which could be literal or figurative...wait a minute or two, maybe even a day or two if possible to process the message. You may find that there is a different meaning that continues to show itself to you that you may have not initially seen or heard. Enjoy your time within the Records as learn to discern the messages, their meanings and the interactive manifestations between the Records, yourself and the rest of your world.

WE AS A TRIBE OR CULTURE HAVE ALWAYS
SOUGHT TO BE MORE AWARE THAN WE ARE.

Chapter 6

WALKING
IN THE
WORLD
EXPANDED

Through our evolutionary patterns we are self conditioned for progress. We are creative beings and we tend toward creating in every moment that we are awake in human form. From smaller whimsical momentary thoughts, feelings actions and ideas to monumental ideas and plans implemented which could change humanity or the world we live in.

In these creative patterns we have also sought to understand ourselves, the Universe and our Creator. To seek out or get closer to heaven by building towers into the sky to be closer to the stars, God and the heavens or to be living in high mountain villages where the energy vibration is higher.

As we have sought to understand God and ourselves on this level we have also immersed ourselves collectively into spiritual and religious studies through history. All the way back to ancient Lemuria and Atlantis. Deep connections with the Earth and nature. As the ancient Hindu tribes and culture studied advanced spirituality through the yogas great strides were made in achieving spiritual powers and insights. The Buddhist and pre-Buddhist monks of Tibet, Japan, and the Far East had many unique was of mastery with nature and within there own selves.

We as a tribe or culture have always sought to be more aware than we are. As we came to master bi-location, levitation, instant manifestation, viewing into the future, and even healing others and ourselves in the spiritual tribes and temples, we have forgotten probably way more than we remember. If we were naturally operating at these levels think of how much farther along we might be as a race. To be more loving and respectful and living in alignment with nature and the Earth could be powerfully magical all by itself. Listening to the Earth and all of nature allows for the Earth and all of nature to be listening to us as a group consciousness.

As we come forward in time to current events, the great thing about personal self development is that it is in direct alignment with our tendency to evolve and create. Knowing this in and of itself can help someone move forward be giving them the inner wisdom or creative balance to persevere in their studies.

As you move forward in your studies, your energy

will be changing and opening if it hasn't already. We go through a series of different shifts as we continue our spiritual studies. For some of us it is enough to exist within our lives just as we are and contemplate new levels of awareness. This is a gentler approach than what others experience. Some of us are on the fast track to realization or enlightenment.

As soon as we get to a certain level we desire to move forward by advancing to a new expression of energetic awareness. This can be due to a Soul contract of spiritual development or simply a burning desire to learn more about the ways in which everything works and our participation with it, as we discover just how far we can go.

As we continue our 'wake up' process we ebb and flow daily even at heightened levels of awareness. We tend to expand to a certain level of energy and then sometimes forget that we have advanced to a new energy level because we become so used to being in it. It may be helpful to take a moment to think back to other times in your life. Maybe you had more energy to burn though maybe you were also operating at lower levels of the ego. Take a moment to be grateful for all of the different shifts that you have been through energetically.

This may take more than a few moments. Think of the momentary shifts and the life changing 'no turning back' transformative shifts. As you take some time to contemplate these times in your world there are two points of awareness that you will naturally arrive at:

A. You are definitely different or changed

B. You are interestingly enough still the same person.

Funny how that works isn't it? After all of the work and the changes we've been, we are still the same Soul enjoined with the same body. Though you also now know that you are changed through your life experiences and your energetic and spiritual studies. You may never be quite the same.

Some of us are already awakened and expanded as the result of a trauma in life, an illness or even a near death situation. In cases such as these individuals often seek a point of reference or an understanding as to why their internal energy, energy fields, and sensations within the body and mind are so different than what they might perceive as the ways that others in the world around them are processing energy in life and the world. Some of these individuals know that they are in an expanded state and have come to accept it and are able to navigate life in a functional way. Others may constantly spiral through moment to moment and day to day asking of life and the Universe for some sort of a representational reference in order to understand their place within it all.

Another dynamic that occurs is that someone may be gradually or consistently opening and incrementally increasing their energy and then at some point there is a dramatic shift that occurs and plunges them forward into unknown territory. This can create a lapse of reason in everything that an individual knows from their life values, perspective and continued work ethic.

While all of these possible scenarios and the personal story of opening may be and probably is unique to the Self, the Earth energy has been incrementally increasing and not necessarily consistently. As the earth continues into the great photonic field, there are astrological occurrences that add to strength of the shifts that may occur. Single or multiple planets in retrograde, full moons on auspicious dates, comets and asteroids coming close to the earth, solar flares, solar and lunar eclipses and any of these occurring at the same time.

Living and existing in these current changing times requires us to find our balance more so than ever before. You may find that you are not able to indulge in the same diet that you once were able to 'slide under the radar' with. Some of these energetic energy shifts may have us seeking to find our own balance anywhere from a few hours, days, months or years. When shifts occur we are required to live our lives differently.

Sometimes your body needs to adjust to running higher frequencies through it and so you may feel tired instead of supper charged by the higher energy. The key to this is grounding, and breathing. Yoga is a great source of synergizing one's own body and chakras with the Earth and sky. Tai Chi and Qi Gong are also great ways to work with the polarity within and around the body. Mudras and mantras also offer unique properties in influencing the subtle energies for clearing, balancing, healing and manifesting.

As you walk forward in life in a newly expanded way others and the external world may seem to be different. They may have changed to you because of your shift or they may have also been changing of there own accord. One thing that's always pretty consistent is change. We see the world in new ways. When we now know who we are and who we have been and what we are capable of, the playing field and the players seem to change in our perception of them.

If we can stay balanced and stay grounded as we continue to open, one of the greatest things we can offer to ourselves and to others is compassion. We may see others' path as very different from our own. If we are moving forward and others are seemingly stationary in their life this may require compassion. Likewise if others are moving forward and we are seemingly stationary this may also require compassion.

As your energy continues to shift you will come

to understand through perception or even trial and error that your thoughts words and deeds now pack more of a punch. You may need to meter or gauge your interactions with others and what you put out into the world.

Often times many of us have wished to be fully expanded until it happens and then may find ourselves playing catch up in order to balance the more expanded levels of energy exchange.

Some have become more psychically opened while others may be having increased sensitivity levels in the empathic field. Having a **kundalini** activation within the body and it's chakras can be a very spiritual experience for those who have been preparing for lengths of time in order to be able to comfortably seat this energy within the body. For anyone unprepared for a kundalini awakening, this is something that could play havoc in the interactions between a person and their surroundings as well as within the body.

There are those that are able to step into it without preparation. The number of people that feel an unbridled continual surging energy and are not sure where it is going or what will happen next is far greater than those who open naturally and are flowing with it having no direction or training. We would hope that expansion would be more comfortable. There are adjustments and balances that have to be made when we experience a shift or change of this nature. It is an advance level of energy activation and should be proceeded with caution and care. This is why in India that people prepare for many years to have a kundalini awakening, sometimes their whole lives.

As you continue your Akashic Records work, one thing that will continually grow for you is your natural psychic awareness. You may feel it coming on when you are not aware of it. You will also get flashes intuitively about people or events. Often times you may not be able to do anything with the information simply because you can't walk up to friends, family of strangers and blurt out psychic messages from beyond that may create life changing or karmic events for them in their lives. So instead you can wait and observe the right moment when you might say something that is more of a generally remote remark that would give the other person something to think about in relation to things in their lives. As you start to operate at heightened levels of seeing and awareness take good care in your approach with others and the rest of the world.

YOGA, DIET, MEDITATION, CLEANSING, FORGIVENESS, GRATITUDE, HEALING, EXERCISE AND EVERY OTHER THING THAT IS POSITIVE THAT YOU CAN DO ARE ALL INTERACTIVE PORTALS WAITING FOR YOU AS YOU CREATE YOUR SACRED SPACE WITHIN.

Chapter 7

CREATING SACRED SPACE TO WORK WITHIN YOUR HOME & SELF

*A*s you continue to learn and study the Akashic Records and other things related with the spiritual playing field, you will find yourself naturally changing some of your preferences in life. As you change, grow and learn your surroundings will start to change as well. You will find that some of your acquaintances and possibly even some long standing relationships may fall away or take a back seat to your new life.

Shifting energetically or spiritually may cause others to question our personal integrity, sanity and life in general as we forge forward into uncharted waters. These rifts between the new and the old can create questions or conflict for us as well as others. We may blame it on our new found spiritual studies though if you think about it, these shifts can occur between people with or without spiritual shifts. Often life changes will take place whether or not spirituality is involved. So when we shift our world shifts. Sometimes we try to normalize our life by continuing in our old patterns. This can prove to be uncomfortable though it doesn't have to be. Everyone's lives are different. Change comes easier for some and they flow with it, while others sometimes may experience turbulence while figuring everything out on the playing field of life.

As you experience shifts your preferences for food and diet may change. You may find yourself eating lighter and/or better quality of foods. You may find that everything from your personal belongings to the area in which you live now is very different or in the process of changing.

As you are studying this Akashic material may I suggest to you that you designate a place within your home or living space to your practice. Maybe you have a special chair that you like to sit in or a part of the house that you are used to feeling inspired or creative in. You may already have a space that you use for meditation.

As you continue to do the Akashic Records work it will be important for you to clear your space and to keep it clear. There are several ways that you can do this. You can use sage to smudge the airspace, windows, doors and mirrors in your house. A smudge stick can be found online or at a local spiritual shop unless you make your own. Make sure that your smoke alarms are turned off, light the sage and burn it until it is flowing through the air. This clears out all unwanted astral activity. Clear your own energy fields around your body as well. If you can't light sage you can at least have it present in the home. Saying sacred prayers of clearing, blessings and good tidings are important to designate your space as sacred space. As you continue to do this, God, Mother Earth, your Guides the Angels and the Masters are all listening and your space will be protected.

Working with crystals is another way to ground in the spiritual energy and clear higher vibrations into your sacred space. Make sure that if you have a collection of crystals that has been sitting in your space for a long period of time that you take them and submerse them in a tub full of salt water or in the sun or both. Another little known way of clearing a crystal is to put it in the freezer. Burying them in sand or a bowl of salt for at least 1-2 days is good. If you are an energy worker and these are in your space where you work with others I recommend clearing the crystals you use in session periodically. Besides the energy it will also give to you creative energy and help with the aesthetics of your living or working space.

Crystals can be a naturally uplifting element in that they give off positive energy in ways that gives to you and also gives to others who enter your space as well as to the space and to the Earth itself.

Using positively inspiring and uplifting artwork in the space you are creating can be a key element for shifting the energy in your space. You may even consider changing the wall colors to something a little more lighter and brighter. Also keeping your airspace pure and clear will benefit you and your space greatly. A fresh breath of inspiration when you walk into a room is what you want to feel.

Ultimately the greatest benefactor to your dream space and your vision is going to be the energy that you put into it. So as you continue to meditate on Love, Gratitude, Prosperity and Healing, the energy of your meditations and energy exercises will infuse your space. You will be able to feel it within the space and when you go out into the world and return home you will feel it even more. In this way you are creating a sacred space.

As you transform your space you are transforming the world around you. This has also the power to transform the space within you. To designate your Sacred Inner Space. As you are working in this new level you are stepping into the flow of Sacred Space, Healing and Ever New Creative Possibilities! You may now continually blossom on new levels of ever changing and always giving new ways of living your life.

This is the spiritual journey of creating sacred space within yourself. Getting to a place within one's self where there is clarity, creativity, love and prosperity is a place of balance. Riding that wave of balance in today's world is the key to sustained happiness and success. When you find these moments and these feelings remember it. Make a mental note of these moments because you will want to study them and recreate them in ever new ways within new moments, hours, days, weeks, months and the years of your life. I recommend as you have an inspired moment to manifest more of these blossoming moments. You may find different ways within yourself to sit down and to get into this groove.

Another way is to think of this moment as a perfect oasis that you travel to in thought as often as possible. As you continue to do this you are making a series of thoughts that will mend themselves together more frequently in your moment to moments of linear time.

The same dynamic is true with the visualization of a rock or a foundation that you may mentally step onto. In this image your rock or foundation is your peaceful, prosperous, loving, streaming moment. Any elements of visualization that you create for yourself that are effective are worth using. Keep remembering back to that moment, back to the moment that felt good and inspired you! Where everything felt better than just okay. Where you glimpsed your greatness. Yoga, diet, meditation, cleansing, forgiveness, gratitude, healing, exercise and every other thing that is positive that you can do are all interactive portals waiting for you as you create your Sacred Space within.

The next message could have been written in a few of the other chapters 'Time Travel, Heightened Levels of Seeing, or How the Energy of the Akasha works.' The truth is that this is how the Universal energy works and I want to address it here in relation to you creating your Sacred space within and your perception of the Divine.

As you go within to create your sacred space within your self and your home and you are walking in the world expanded now. As you sense into the energy of time and space an ancient proverb is something for you to consider here. "The Tao that can be named is not the true Toa." What does this mean? There are so many ancient proverbs which beg us to open our minds to greater awareness. Another like this is: 'To be on the Path you must first become the Path'. Very similar though there are some unique differences.

Back to the Tao statement. 'The Tao that can be named is not the true Toa. A great yogi from India, Babaji, had made a statement similar to this in another way. Remember the designation of God and the Universal in the here and now operating through you as 'I Am That I Am'. Babaji has stated "I Am That" giving an open end or an elusiveness to the compression of his statement. Is this the Tao that can not be named? I say yes.

As you go within and you look between the moments for the Tao. Oops we've designated it. Back up and look between those moments or between the spaces between the moments. Oops we've designated again. Keep looking and go deeper. You will find the place of no meaning and no names.

This is a common problem of perception for us physical humans because we are in a seemingly separate container and yet we know we are all connected through a oneness. Actually there are different levels of the Oneness. We are one with the collective consciousness of humanity. We are one with all life upon the Earth and we are one with the Universal Mind of God. So which level of Oneness would you like to be part of today?

This could also be a unique study in enlightenment or self realization. As you study the vastness of spirit, the world, the Universe and your place within it all you are awakening to new levels of understanding and Truth. This will help you in your Akashic Records studies of non-judgment and releasing all conflicts within yourself as you learn to go deeper in search for your greater Self Knowing within the Records.

THIS IS THE PLACE WHERE SOULS LEARN ABOUT THEIR LIFE LESSONS AND KARMAS, THEIR GREATEST TRIUMPHS AND THEIR MISSED OPPORTUNITIES. THIS IS A PLACE OF STUDY AND IT IS VERY WELL PROTECTED BY THE HIGHER BEINGS.

Chapter 8

HOW THE ENERGY OF THE AKASHA WORKS

The Akashic Records is interactive. As we start to practice our journeys into the Records our meditations are a way for us to connect into the interactive library that will stream information to us through our Soul and through our mind's eye. So we continue to take in more information about this Great Library and our sense of the energies that run through and surround it.

One element is paramount to your inquiries into the Records and that is reverence. We do not go into God's library of Souls and attempt to hack information about another person for worldly gain or any covert reasons. In fact this living library will shut you down when it is approached from lower levels of the ego. Many people have tried and usually what happens is that they are directed to a fail safe astral version of the Records that will give them facsimiles of what they are searching for. Trying to use the Akashic Records for lower levels of information is like searching for a haystack within the needle. It just doesn't work.

Conspiracy based inquiries which may be riddled with drama will usually get a person skewed information at best. You may want to consult another source. So with all levels of all information about all things is available here then why can't we interact with the Akasha as we see fit for whatever we want? The fist directive to getting any good, clear and useful information is going to be releasing all conflicts, fears, doubts and preconceived notions. And again we are in one of Creator's Universal Libraries of Souls and reverence is the key word here. This is the place where the Masters and the Arc Angels come and work with Souls as well as the Keeper's of the Records. So let's also have a little respect and patience.

This is the place where Souls learn about their life lessons and karmas, their greatest triumphs and their missed opportunities. This is a place of study and it is very well protected by the higher beings. So let me ask you now, what is your intention for receiving information and knowledge from the

Records? If your intention is truly of the Light then you may enter and have access to these great banks of knowledge.

When you are operating from a place of goodness, you will always have access to the higher information because they already know that you are trustworthy with it.

Let's talk about space time events within the Akashic Records and how our reality relates to this. As we had discussed in an earlier chapter the messages from the Akasha can be either literal or figurative or both. An event that is written within the Book of Life within God's library can play itself out in multiple ways. It could even have an enumerable measure of response pattern. This is because the event exists and it's waiting for your interactive response or participation in order to play out the event in creation.

As an example: You may think about leaving from your home to go to the store for some groceries.

Question: How many different routes could you take to get from your home to the store even it meant going entirely around the world?

Do you see now the immeasurable different ways in which you could go from point A to point B? This is also the way the energy works from the Akasha in reference to 3D reality space-time events. So we may be going in our life in a certain direction to do something and Creator, the Universe, the world, our guides, or our own preferred responses or conditioning may take us around the world in order to arrive at the same or similar outcome or destination.

In one view point you may choose to see all the extra work involved that could have been avoided. From another view point you may acknowledge the experience of and the experience gained from going all the way around the world. As you get into touch with this dynamic you will start to process and understand on a higher level the way that things can play out.

Often when we think we have a translation based on our observations I recommend waiting a little while because other perspectives may present themselves during the process of more introspection. This is when you really start to understand that variables and forces are at work other than just your own actions or intellectual response to any given event or series of events.

Another element to consider is that just because the prophecy or event is given from the Records does not mean that it is undeniably set in stone. Prophecies were originally given so that they do not have to come true. Though this is almost never the case when dealing with the ego of an individual or groups. The ego often wants to 'take the bait' so to speak, without questioning. A good example of this would be the apocalypse or the 'last days' as many have tried to literally interpret from the Book of Revelations in the Holy Bible. Another would be an earthquake or tsunami that could destroy the California coast. So many have predicted this and even seen visions of it. Are these and many other events set in stone? Was it ever meant to be interpreted literally or figuratively? And Ultimately does this really have to happen? These are questions that petition us for deeper observation as opposed to simple yes and no answers.

One perspective might be, that just as in seeing a possible coming event of an individual and changing one's actions in order to avoid karma or greatly alter the event altogether. Responding to a coming event as a culture might involve planetary cleanup or working more with nature. Mother Earth is listening and when the karma and emotional and mental discharges from the billions of people living here are starting to be cleared then we are creating a different outcome.

Let's talk about the nature of the Soul and how it works with the Akashic Energy. Your Soul's energy is Divine. It is Celestial. It is a part of God's Soul. As the Creator released parts of His/Her/Itself across all of the Universes our Souls are actual fingerprints of God's energy. This is in part why there has come to be a demand for Soul energy between the Light and Dark. You might say it's become the ultimate currency. This God energy has the ability to be imprinted with greatness through creativity, love, passion, truth, and many other great aspects. Your Soul is a majestic being. As we become more whole again we often are able to simplify our life in ways that permit us to see this connection to our own greatness.

The fact that we are a Celestial Soul enjoined with a physical human body that is bringing our conscious awareness through this body into this reality *is the miracle*. Read the last sentence again and meditate on it for a few moments. As you study how the body is keeping itself alive with the aid of this Divine Consciousness our priorities may change.

As you change your perspective of the relationship between the Soul and human body you start to realize a greater purpose. And this also changes the way the energy itself responds with you. The nature of the Soul is to live in harmony with the Divine. The Souls have a Divine harmonic connection with the coinciding Books of Life for each Soul within the Great Hall of Records.

This is more than a library, it is a divinely organic interactive home or way station for all Souls. Your Soul is enjoined through you body. It is radiating into your physical body and out from your physical body simultaneously. As this continues the Soul is also connected up into the higher dimensions to your Book of Life in the heavenly realm of the Akasha. This is where everything that you experience here on Earth is written down and stored energetically and harmonically.

There is an upload stream and a download stream connect to each one of us through our crown. We are all uploading or inputting information about our journey into our Books of Life continuously. Through history fewer of us have had access to download the information individually or to study other information within the Records though it is possible for everyone.

As we practice connecting into the Akashic Records there are other dynamics at play. There are energetic gifts that can be received by osmosis just from consciously being in the Records and working with them. After a time that you have been doing this work you may come to feel, understand or know that your karma is changing. For two reasons:

A. By doing the work of Self understanding you are becoming a Self Knowing being or a Self Realized being, so you are shifting your own personal karma.

B. Spending time in the Akasha can also have transformative vibrational effects which can naturally remove and clear certain levels of karma.

This is similar to being in the presence of a Great Spiritual Master. The energy vibrations are transformational.

Much in the same way we are able to also receive certain levels of physical healing as well as Soul Healing. This is huge. As you revisit the Akashic Records you will also be clearing, healing and balancing your other lifetimes whether you are working directly with them or by osmosis.

So in time as you continue this work you will be shifting in subtle ways you never thought possible. Now I don't want you to think that you will be receiving a magical cure just by visiting the Records. I do not wish to convey any such fix-it-quick schemes. There is too much of this going on in today's metaphysics in an attempt to energetically shift on a quantum level, and some of these new ways do work.

I want you to study the classic energetic and meditation ways of entering into the Akashic Records and with the right reasons and intention in your heart and mind in order to receive any other positive effects that can occur as a result of right use and right study.

If you are studying creatively as a visual artist, composer or some other form of art, you will find the energy of the Akasha very interactive and very giving to you. As you go into an Akashic meditation and you focus on a certain art form you are creating you may receive much information about this creation. It may come alive and show itself to you as it creates itself before you, showing you options and different approaches. Never ending and always beginning, The Akasha is a vastly rich source for artists, inventors and all creative types. This is the cocreative Source Light and Cosmic Energy of Creation.

The same may be true with the healing arts. There are many modern day modalities that have come through to people like you and me to be shared with the world. These are actually being downloaded for these individuals from the Akashic Records via their guides, the masters and the angels.

As you continue to study the energy of the Akashic Records and how it interactively works you will also become creatively aware of the possibilities in relation to manifesting different versions of your reality.

I highly recommend never to go into your Book of Life and rewrite the protocols that your Soul has set up for you. I mention this because it is a question that has often come up in the workshops. Have people tried this? Yes. Is it a virtuous practice to go in and try to shift or cheat life in this way by taking a shortcut? Not really. There can be major karmic repercussions in this life and in the afterlife as a result of tampering on this level. You could be moving karmic events set up for you to other times in your life or just postponing events which were meant for you to have a response to.

Now if you are making new choices and your life has shifted drastically and you have been doing multitudes of karma clearing and service work, then you will be shifting the Records naturally. If you are in a position of this nature the consideration to work with your Records on this interactive level might be an option without repercussions. You will want to go in and ask or pray about it and listen for guidance as to the best way to proceed. Your Higher Self and guides already know what the best answer is.

Naturally going into the Akashic Records with humble reverence is always your best calling card. You will receive so much more by not creating any more conflicts than the ego might already have. As you continue viewing from your own personal Records you will now get new ways of doing things, new creative ventures and ideas, and even new approaches to life. This will given you a natural inside curve on upping your own life game of manifesting a better life for yourself and achieving your goals.

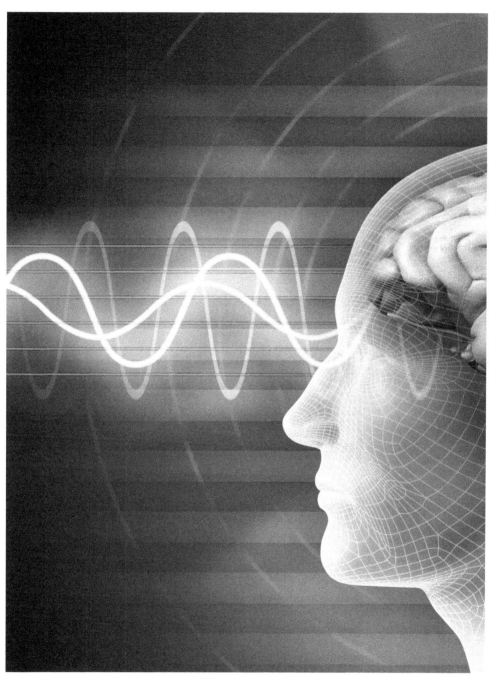

HEALING WITH QUANTUM ENERGY IS A WAY OF BYPASSING THE DENSITY OF THE PHYSICAL BODY AND MEETING IT IN QUANTUM DIMENSIONS WHILE SURPASSING THE PHYSICAL AND THEN TRANSLATING THE HEALING BACK INTO THE PHYSICAL PLANE

Chapter 9

USING THE AKASHIC RECORDS AS A MEDICAL INTUITIVE

*A*cross the world through history we have wondered of our own origins. As we continued to use our brilliant minds over the course of time as a race we have created so much within our cultures. The Arts, Music, Poetry, Science, and Healing. Healing has been a mainstay since our beginnings. As we became civilized, we grew, learned and studied. One thing that has always been of immediate concern is that of our physical well being. Recovering from injuries of all sorts whether related to work, play, hunting, war, personal combat, travel epidemics and the list goes on.

The tribes have always had **Shamans** to work for clearing and healing a persons Soul. When someone was missing parts of their Soul through life's series of challenging events, they would go to the shaman of the tribe who would perform a spiritual ritual for them. This often involved journeying from the present into alternate realities known as the upper, middle and lower worlds to retrieve missing pieces of a person's Soul.

Bringing the Soul back to a person could fill them up and make them feel whole, balanced and grounded again. Often when the Soul fully returns it positively affects a person bringing support and energetic peace on a Soul level in ways that cannot be achieved otherwise.

This is also an affective procedure in today's world especially with our modern complex lives which include all of our emotional and mental calisthenics. This ancient form of healing is not only effective but also necessary at times when modern medicine cannot fully help someone who is suffering from a disconnection of their own soul energy.

This involves the Shaman going into a trance or a deep meditation and traveling to these other worlds which are known as **Shamanic State of Consciousness.** This is something that can't often be done any other way.

The similarity to this and all other forms of healing procedures is the dynamic of one person providing healing technique of some sort in care and service to another person. Often it is necessary in energetic procedures just as in medical procedures to have another person providing care to the self. In energetic procedures of healing you will find that it can be quite a bit more affective to have someone other than yourself administering the energy healing.

It is important to always run the cosmic energy of healing for one's self in order to always keep the presence of energy available to us. It is in great times of need that another person may be more effective with the directing of energy through one's body.

Throughout history one of the world's oldest professions has been that of fortune telling, prophecy or foretelling the future, contacting God, the angels and others in the higher realms, etc. These were the beginnings of psychic phenomena for the human race. As we learned to develop our mystical nature, we grew and naturally became more psychic. Our physiology and energy systems was already set up to be continuously psychic as demonstrated over time by the Atlanteans, the masters of India and other great minds such as DiVinchi, Nostradamus, Swedenborg and Cayce.

Now if we travel back in time before the last deluge the advanced humans were very psychic and telepathic. All were connected with nature through the Earth and ethers as one. These were the times of Atlantis. In this time there were several variations of humans on the planet at the same time which we will go into later.

Over the course of history there are stories of angels, beings from on high, ascended healers, Christ Jesus and even God appearing to people and bringing healing energy that in many cases brought an instantaneous or miraculous healing to them. This is a transference of healing energies brought to a person from other dimensions just outside our own to affect a person's physical well being with healing or the surrounding situation of their life. This was and still is often looked at as miraculous and wondrous.

Psychic Surgery is a term that has been used to explain the phenomena of healers from South America such as the practitioners of Spiritism. This is the act of a healer becoming empowered from the other side by way of a healing spirit that gifts both the healer and patient with a surgical procedure in which either common household tools or the bare hands of the healer are used. In these operations there is zero pain felt by the patient in each case. This probably sprang forth out of need in times and in parts of the world where modern medicine or procedures were not available. At any rate the healings that have been documented are nothing short of miraculous. Again another form of spiritual energy working with or through a healer here in the physical world to help others.

There have been many modern modalities of energy healing spring forth into circulation in the last several decades including Reiki, Reconnection Healing, Quantum Touch, Matrix Energetics, Theta Healing and the list goes on.

One type of healing that is a more modern approach is both the product of the ancient techniques handed down and in a new frontier all in it's own is what has come to be known as **Medical Intuitive Healing**.

Medical Intuitive Healing is the study which I believe came into existence as a result of the earlier work of a great 1900's psychic by the name of Edgar Cayce which primarily used his gifts to help others in the form of intuitive counseling and diagnosis of countless thousands of individuals which received help. Edgar Cayce was also responsible for coining the phrase "Akashic Records" as a result of studying the early works of Immanuel Swedenborg and having also a natural gift which went well beyond his practical thinking mind in the ways of connecting into the Akasha and retrieving great wealths of helpful information for individuals in his lifelong service. His gifts also came at a time in a small town in Kentucky when there was a need for medical help in the area where he grew up which was meager and lacked much of any medical resources for miles.

An even older version or term used to describe what we are talking about may have sprang forth in earlier centuries in Europe and termed as **Psychic Healing**. So as many of the people using this term in previous centuries may have had a similar and in some ways a more direct approach to the practice of projecting energy. Similar in nature and yet different. The term even has a different energy to it. We will cover Psychic Healing with an exercise in the Workbook.

So as a continuing result today we have the new phenomena of those who are studying and practicing intuitively in giving information to others concerning health matters by way of connecting with guides or by directly 'vibing in' to what is going on within a person's body. Medical Intuitives can either diagnose or diagnose and proceed to heal.

As a medical intuitive proceeds to heal there are many different creative approaches that can be taken.

Here are some ways of Medical Intuitive Healing that may include but are not limited to:

1. Connecting with a persons guides and working directly with them to heal a person.
2. Connecting with a person's Soul and assisting the Soul energy in repairing the body.

3. Working on specific areas of a person's body through the coinciding astral body as this will then be translated into the physical.

4. Healing with Quantum energy is a way of bypassing the density of the physical body and meeting it in quantum dimensions while surpassing the physical and then translating the healing back into the physical plane.

5. It is also possible for some healers to travel into a person's body to look at what is wrong and to make repairs by directing healing energy with the mind in a surgical procedure.

6. It is possible to call forth a blue print or a 3-D holographic representation of a person's body, spirit and energetic makeup and then to make changes form the projection and then placing it back within a person.

You may already get empathic feelings from others. These impressions may come as emotions, energy sensations or just feelings in the body including pain or discomforts that others are experiencing. This is a good place to note that all too often healers have had the experience of pulling pain or discomfort from a person's body into their own body or fields as a way of helping the other person. It is well noted that if this dynamic starts to occur make sure that you give it directly back to God or the Universe and do not hold on to it in your body. This will insure a cleaner and more effective way of healing without affecting you afterwards. Always remember to clear yourself before and after each healing.

7. And last, but certainly not the least, you can use the Akashic Records as a multidimensional way of looking into a person's Soul Records and working from this place as a point of reference. As you work from within the Akashic Records and you are with the core essence of a person from this place you can then ask questions concerning a person's health and well being and get multiple levels of information. As you work with a person from within the Records you can affect great clearing, healing and progress for them sometimes on levels that even bypass the physical body though directly affecting it.

Any and all of the aforementioned styles of intuitive healing can be applied and used as you start going into the Records to practice working with a person in order to realign them energetically, mentally, physically, spiritually and physically.

Let's now do an exercise of going into the Records to work with some one. You may call in the higher self of someone that you know needs assistance. You may ask that person if it is okay for you to work with them. If you get a 'yes' then it is okay to proceed. If you get a 'no' that means there is a karmic lesson that person is working with and it is better to take another approach. You may ask a friend if it is okay to work with them as a special healing participant. Or if you are in the class we will work back and forth as partners on each other. When we do this we know that our guides, the angels, the Keepers of the Records and our higher selves all know that we are working for the best and the highest outcome of healing. In this way we are protected.

EXERCISE: MEDICAL INTUITIVE AKASHIC HEALING PRACTICE

Get comfortable as you start to relax. As you prepare to connect into the Akashic Records call all of the guides and healers that you may already be working with. Maybe there is a whole team. Maybe there is just one or a few that have been with you all along. Maybe new healing guides come in for different people. As you continue to relax, let the many aspects of your spiritual being intervene, intercede and come forth with your higher self as you start to project yourself into the Records. You may open a portal of white light and start to venture up into the **Akashic Hall of Healing Wisdom**.

Or you may open the portal of White Light as everything else in the room grows dimmer and the Hall of Healing Wisdom now comes into view as it appears around you. As this happens and you find yourself in the Healing Hall, now call the higher self of the person which you wish help. As they are in front of you and you greet them, kindly ask them to tell you what is going on within there body and/or mind & emotions.

Listen closely to what they are sharing with you. You may also at this time look into the energetic blue-print of their physiology. As you look into them ask your guides and the Records Keepers to show you the spots in colors or light that are needing attention. As you see what needs attention and you are practicing this new method of healing, you may ask again 'What is the best approach to affect change within this person for their highest healing?'

As they give you the answers you may find that as you proceed you are either using a technique of healing that you are used to or it could be something completely different and new to you. As you continue your journey of healing they may help you to realize many new and creatively colorful ways of directing healing for a person.

As you continue practicing you will accomplish many things. You will have many attempts and procedures of healing that you turn over to the Universe and to the person you are working with as you are just a tool or a vessel for the energy of healing to flow through to reach the other person.

When you do this you are connected to Spirit and listening and operating in your highest capacity. You are involved and facilitating but ultimately you are not responsible for their healing. That is between them, the Universe and their Creator. So as you utilize your techniques that you are being shown give gratitude and love to everyone involved especially the patient. In the classes and workshops we will be going through every part of the healing processes individually.

Here I want to you to practice creative forms that they (the guides and healers on the other side) are giving to you. In this way you develop an interactive relationship with them and they know you're ready to listen learn and participate at ever greater levels.

As you now complete your process, say a healing prayer for the individual you are working with on all levels as you finish. As you bring them back to their selves the Light of the Akashic Healing Hall of Wisdom now begins to fade and returns you back to the 'here and now' in this present moment.

Thank you Divine Intelligence of the Universe for working through me to bring healing to others. Amen

IN THE ETERNAL NOW THE SOUL IS
PARTICIPATING IN OTHER LIFETIMES
SIMULTANEOUSLY

Chapter 10

AKASHIC SHAMANIC
SEEING, FEELING, KNOWING

*B*eyond a thousand suns and a million waves crashing on the beaches of eternity are the Great Halls of the Akasha and the Shamanic dimensions. In the great depths and heights of our spiritual studies and intuitive adventures exist the very real other worlds. The colorful and unique quests that we have ignited within the spiritual fires of our inner creative mind, body and spirit.

As we look into the Akashic Records we practice from the approach that reverently every journey is an ever knew experience. In this way we are able to cultivate a great amount of colorful information that either sooner or later adds to our wisdom and knowledge. As we learn to continue gaining access in this way we build a new inner world and inner journey. As we go deep into our meditation process when preparing to access the Records we then project ourselves through our conscious awareness travelling up through the senses into the target location of the Hall of Records, God's Library, the Akashic Records.

We access certain vibrations as we visit the Records. We begin to come accustomed to what we will usually feel when we journey into the Records though these frequencies may also vary from time to time. You come to know what to expect. As you have continued practicing your belief and faith in what you are studying and it's approach has yielded results which now bring you to a place of more trusted knowing.

From this trusted knowing you now continue throughout your studies to bring in more information and to also bring a great sense of understanding. This has put you on a new path in life as you now look back and realize what you have done so far in your accomplishments.

Working in the Akasha has a very light and high vibration to it. Everything is of light and in many ways it feels like air. Such are the dynamics of working with the 'sky library'.

As for those who work with the deep earth energies to help others heal their Soul this is another dimensional reference point and place.

While both the Akashic and the Shamanic work to help a person with their Soul in different ways. If you have worked with both of these energies then you may know what I am referring to here.

Let's talk more about the dynamics of Shamanism. This energy is what we consider to be more deeply earth based. In some ways you may have to experience it in order to know what the differences are.

Some individuals or shamans working with them may have or may be using 'plant medicine'. I don't encourage it, though if you or someone else has had an enlightening experience because of it, then you have that is a mind opening experience in which you can compare to our natural and clear journeys to the Records. Your experience may have even add to your progress as you know investigate other dimensional levels of knowing and seeing.

As we talked about in Vol. 1 sometimes after having a hallucinogenic experience people may be drawn to try and recreate an experience over and over which could become a problem. Opening the gateway of the mind by means of an outside source whether natural or not can be tricky. There often is no way to control or gauge the depth or intensity of the experience. For that reason I prescribe doing any journey work 'all naturale'. You can learn to do shamanic journey work and have visions and deep interactions in healing without ingesting any outside substances.

In Shamanism as a person journeys deep within the Earth Spirit there is another set of worlds which can be accessed: the upper, middle and lower worlds. These inter-dimensional worlds are respective in representation of each other. The upper world represents the heavens and the land of light. The middle world represents the physical planes and the lifetimes lived. The lower world represents the land of the dead.

When an individual journeys into these realms you might think of it as similar to the astral plane though it is not. It is a parallel set of dimensions that is specific to the Mother Earth and is there for the purpose specifically around healing. For this reason these realms are rarely accessed by anyone else for any other purposes other than healing. This is very akin to the realm of the Akasha which is used in the same way. Only for the purposes of self healing, Soul Healing intuitive knowledge and wisdom for the healing of karma, and just as in Shamanism, for Soul healing, soul retrieval and body spirit healing.

As someone journeys into the deep earth realms through a 'shamanic state of consciousness' if it is done correctly they are going into the 'in between' these are where these places for healing are located, in between dimensions. The same is true with the true levels of the Akashic Records. This is yet another way in which these places and pathways are protected from those who would use either modality for meddling in lower affairs. I want you to be excited and inspired about accessing the Akashic Records but I also want you to be careful and proceed respectfully. Remember with great knowledge comes great responsibility and you will be the next generation of healers and guides.

As you go into the practice of accessing the Records you do not need to focus on the idea that they or hidden or existing within dimensions, you simply need to relax and allow yourself to be guided past the physical and up through the astral plane or 5th dimension and up into the higher finer places of light where the Records exist. Your Soul knows the way.

With Shamanic work you will be doing the same. As you say your prayers and are guided deep down into the Earth's energy, the worlds of the healers know how to direct you there as much as your intention also takes you there.

I have met several shamans who do not use plant medicine to journey and it is very clear or quiet in their space of healing. I have met other shamans who are using the medicine and their is usually some sort of astral doorway that has a tangible feel. When I feel things like this I usually in my book would think that a clearing would be in order. To each their own. I will say that it is similar to people working psychically that build up a charge of energy no matter where that energy is coming from. Be discerning and always practice clearing. Cleaner and clearer energy and space will always serve you better.

Both Shamanic and Akashic are about the healing of the Soul. Each have unique aspects that in some ways the other doesn't. They are like 2 sisters. Shamanic will have the deep, deep other dimensional earth energies which are unmistakable once you've had a successful connection to them. Akashic energy is a higher clearer finer energy that is like air or the wind and can feel very spatial. Akashic represents the All, the Earth and all of the Souls. So they are both related in the way of Soul healing though similar yet different ends of the spectrums.

So let's say you have been involved in doing Soul Retrieval work for yourself or for someone else. Either you are giving or receiving. You may journey into the other dimensions of shamanic state of consciousness and find pieces and parts of a person's soul that will be able to be brought back by you, for you, or with the aid of animal familiars or animal spirits used in the shamanic work. Animal spirits are asked to participate because they are pure in their being and connect to the Earth and Universe. In this way they are very effective guides and co-workers in the Shamanic worlds. So as you bring back these soul pieces you may find that it is very effective. Is there another piece to the work that may need to be approached from another angle? Sometimes this is the case.

This is why I use the Akashic Records to look at a person's past lifetime cycles and to see if there is something that is tethering them through the Soul from another lifetime. The Soul is timeless and operating in all dimensions and time lines simultaneously. In this way there are multiple connections to every other earth bound lifetime that the Soul has been engaged with through all of it's incarnations.

As this occurs in the Eternal Now streaming on the other side, the Soul is participating in other lifetimes simultaneously. Some of these lifetimes are pulling at the Soul energy as something is occurring that needs attention. Perhaps a lesson or karma is involved. Sometimes there is a trauma such as an accident or sickness taking place. Sometimes there are vows or oaths taken in some form that can impact proceeding lifetimes. From this place, I connect with the Soul through the Records while looking at these lifetimes and ask what can be done to heal, clear or isolate the events from past that could be causing an individual a stump in current life progress.

In some ways if possible I am allowed to isolate these past life events to their own time, I am able to acknowledge their existence while knowing that the Soul is currently working with another physical incarnation and enjoined to a current physical body in the present time and day. As we acknowledge this the other time lines are moved back and into their own perspective while the Soul of the person receiving healing ceases to operate as an open portal beyond the grasp of their own control.

When this is happening to people they often have no reference point to what is going on or any way of practically and even sometimes esoterically finding out what is truly going on. It is only in working with the Akashic Records on a Soul level that a healer may be granted the passport in order to work with a person from this perspective. And it may be specific to any said situation. There may be some situations going on with the Soul in other lives that you are asked or guided not to intervene with. You will want to ask and look in to connect on this level through the Records in order to get a clear picture of how to proceed.

When we are working on this level with the Akashic Records we are doing work that is very muck like that of the Shamanic world, that is why I have termed the work **Akashic-Shamanic**. I have used similar points of reference in working with people in Ancestral Healing which entails healing the family tree and bloodline. Often times there are many emotional issues, karmas, traumas, injuries, tendencies and illnesses which are sometimes organically transmitted through the family DNA in that way handed down to the next generation.

As we are working in this way with the Akashic

Records on behalf of the Soul Essence which is not only enjoined with a person but is their true celestial identity as well. We start to move into new territory, where new ways of healing can be achieved. I often find that when I am working people on this level in session that they often experience unique changes and sensations not only because it's needed and that it's a very different approach, but also because nothing else has worked so far from so many other surface level approaches.

So these are the many new ways of Seeing, Feeling and Knowing that we come to experience and understand as part of our Healing journey whether giving, receiving or observing.

Exercise 2

AKASHIC SHAMANIC JOURNEY

*A*s you relax now, relaxing your whole body. And just start to relax your breath. Relaxing your inhale and your exhale. Breathing long and slow and deep. As you continue to relax, relaxing your toes, your heals, your ankles all completely relaxed. Relaxing now your shins and your calves as your lower legs become relaxed and at ease. As this relaxing energy moves up through your knees. Your knees and space behind your knees are completely relaxed and at ease.

At this time as you feel this relaxing energy moving up over your thighs, the front, back, and the sides all relaxed. As the hamstrings and the psoas muscles all completely relaxed and at ease. As you continue to breathe in and out in long slow and gentle deep breaths....

....(yogic kriya breath)....Relax now your hips, waist, your pelvis and your buttocks all completely relaxed as the energy of the base chakra relaxes with it's center at the tailbone of the spine.

Relaxing now your lower back and your lower stomach all completely relaxed. Relaxing your torso, chest and all of the organs within, as you relax down, down, down even deeper. And now as you continue to relax, relaxing ever so gently, ever so deeply, relaxing down, down, down relaxing even deeper.

Your whole body just becomes loose and limp and lazy. Relaxing your shoulders, your mid back and your upper back all completely relaxed. Relaxing now your upper arms, your biceps and your triceps. Your elbows, your forearms, your wrists, your hands, fingers and thumbs all relaxed.

Your palms are open as they are loose and limp and lazy. As you relax down, down, down, relaxing down even deeper. As this great spiritual wave of energy that's moving over your whole body moving up now through your neck and through the back of your head.

As this energy moves up the back of the head and now over the top of the head, this Divine spiritual energy, this relaxing energy moves down washing over the sides of your head and your ears, washing over your forehead and your eye brows. your eyes and your eye sockets all completely relaxed.

Continuing to relax...it washes down over your nose and washes down over your cheeks. Washing now over your mouth, your teeth, your tongue, your gums and your lips all completely relaxed. Relaxed and at ease, relaxing your jaws. Relaxing your throat. Your whole body is relaxed very deeply. Relaxing down, down, down even deeper.

As you relax down even deeper. And as you continue to breathe, there is a great golden ball of light as bright as the sun that is starting to form over your solar plexus. And this is your Light this great golden Light is growing brighter than the sun. And as it continues to grow bright it moves and expands out until it engulfs your body and it lights up the whole room that you are in with no shadows.

So bright...and as it continues to grow bright and expand, this is your Light. And your light continues to expand out past the walls of the room continuing to expand out. Past your home as this great Light, your light, expands out it engulfs the local neighborhood.

Your light continues to expand out until it engulfs the whole area in which you are living, the town or the city or the countryside. Continuing to expand out until it expands across the whole state or providence in which you reside. Expanding and continuing to expand out until it engulfs the complete country in which you live. As your light expands out around the world. It covers now all of North America, covering Canada, the United States, Mexico, Central and South America. Until the whole Western hemisphere is shining very brightly in your Light.

As it expands now out across the ocean and out across Scandinavia and Europe, the United Kingdom, all of these places are shining very brightly with your Light. As the energy continues to expand now and increase your energy engulfs all of Africa and all of the Middle East, continuing to expand out now. Engulfing Russia and the Far East. Engulfing China and Japan. As your Light is so bright engulfing now Australia. Until the whole Eastern hemisphere is shining very brightly in your Light.

Your Light has completely now engulfed the whole world. The whole planet earth is shining very brightly in your Light. And as the world is shining very brightly in your Light you may have noticed that you have ascended up over the planet. As as you are now here looking down at the planet from here in the space of the upper atmosphere.

You are watching the Earth rotate very slowly, seeing all of the countries, all of the oceans all of the weather patterns as they are shining in your Light. And as you are ascended up over the planet you notice now that there are some tiny pinpoints of red light that start to appear and glow in many of the continents in different parts of the world.

And as these red lights glow in different places on the surface. Just take a few moments to survey all of these places...*pause for a moment*...These were places that you lived before in other lifetimes.

These red lights may also indicate certain places on the planet that you have visited in this lifetime where you had interactions, as you continue now to take a few moments to look at these red lights. And now as you've connected with these pinpoints of red light, surveying the surface of the earth, turn your attention now towards the Sun.

Look now directly into the sun in your mind. As you look directly into the great light of the sun and the great loving Divine Intelligence of the solar power itself beaming down into your eyes and into your third eye. Streaming into your crown chakra, into your throat and into your heart, down throughout your body and all of your chakra system. You feel very warm in this powerful light of the sun. You can feel the brilliance and the energy. As it lifts you up it expands your whole body and your whole being.

As this continues the earth energy is coming up and entering in through the bottoms of your feet. Soothing you with deep energy and this energy is grounding you through all of your meridians and chakras. Along with the solar energy, both of these energies are meeting and crossing in all of the chakras and all of the meridians of your body. Healing, balancing and energizing you. Healing balancing and energizing you.

As you continue here between the Sun and the Earth. At this time you spread out your arms in your mind like great wings and as you do this you start to fly in great counter clockwise circles. Down towards the earth. Feel how freeing this is. As you sail, soar, glide and fly continually down, down, down. Flying down, sailing down in great circular patterns. As you continue sailing down towards the planet. The oceans and the continents become brighter and clearer. As you're sailing and soaring down in the great circles descending now closer to the planet.

And as you continue to soar down you find yourself gliding down over North America. And you find yourself sailing and soaring down over the South West. As you are circling now the area of Arizona, New Mexico, Colorado and Utah and the Sacred Four Corners. Continuing to circle you come down to the Four Corners of these states. To the great Native American designation of the Four Corners.

And as you circle and glide down you land there on the Four Corners. And as you land, there is a great Native Sage that is waiting for you. A great Native American medicine man. He's wearing a great white long fringed coat. His name is White Eagle. He is a very tall man with long dark hair. He is very gentle and kindly. And as he greets you holding a great staff he welcomes you to the Four Corners.

"Welcome my dear child to these great Four Corners of Healing. The Spirit of the North, the Spirit of the East, the Spirit of the South, the Spirit of the West have brought you here to heal your Body, to heal your Mind, to heal your Heart and to heal your Spirit. Each of the Four Directions will attend to each part of you. As you take a few moments here to allow the energy of the Four Directions to enter in and to work with you on all levels...*pause for a moment*...You now continue to heal as you have set foot upon this journey to experience the reintegration and to experience the healing of your Soul."

"You have traveled a great distance to be here and we commend you. For your journey is only just beginning. We will guide you we will help to show you the way to heal your Soul, your Heart, Mind, your Body and your Spirit with the Four Directions. As for now come with me my child and let us walk together down this path, down the red road."

And so you start walking along with White Eagle as he continues to joyfully impart wisdom and stories that are gentle and they make you feel so comfortable within yourself.

Here within the Southwest not a care in the world. You are on an adventure, a journey. And as you start walking in the direction of the southwest with White Eagle you find that you are both taking very large strides. As you are taking these very large strides, time and space are both shifting once again. Before you know it you are arriving at the great rim of the Grand Canyon which seemed like just a few miles journey you both made so easily.

As you arrive and you stand side by side with White Eagle looking out over the ancient land and the sacred canyon that helps your soul and your Spirit to expand. It helps you to step into your own greatness. As you continue to expand into your own energy looking out across the vastness of the Grand Canyon. White Eagle now addresses you and says "A Dear Friend is coming from very far away and is coming here to help you continue your journey.

As White Eagle points his staff up to the stars there is a bright light amongst the stars and one of the stars is moving. As it continues to move around and vibrate it becomes larger and larger. This sphere of celestial energy starts to become more visible as it comes closer down to the earth terrain. This sphere, this vehicle of light is a great spiritual saint coming to the Earth plain.

As the sphere comes all the way down and lands beside you, the great sphere of light now transforms into the great master from India, maha avatar Babaji Nagaraj. As Babaji is standing before you as a great friend, as a healer and as a teacher he is here for your journey.

As you greet him he says "Welcome Dear One,

you've traveled far to meet me here and know this, your journey has only just begun. As he continues to visit with you now, you can now feel his energy starting to transform you and change you. There is a great light and a great power that is lifting your body up as it feels full of light and full of strength and yet empty at the same time.

Looking at you and pointing he says "What is this heavy bag that you've been carrying over your shoulder? What is this heavy burden that you have been carrying all of the years and all of these miles?" And as Babaji is looking at you suddenly it dawns on you that you have been carrying this heavy load, this burden all along. You did not realize it until he mentioned it to you. Once he had spoke of it, the heavy bag now became visible over your shoulder.

This bag is filled with many gathered sorrows, resentments and fears, disappointments, karmas and challenging situations with others. Things that were deciding moments for you in your life. They sculpted or carved out of intention and of reality the ways that you would respond to the world.

And now as Babaji asks you politely "Please give me the bag, let me take this burden from you." As you reach over your shoulder you realize just how heavy these burdens have been as you hand this bag over to Babaji. And as he takes it from you, to him it is very light and he flings it down on the ground behind him.

And as he points to the bag with his finger there on the edge of the rim of the Grand Canyon, it becomes on fire. It becomes lit up with the spiritual fire of cleansing karma. The spiritual fire cleanses the karma and burns the heavy burdens.

Babaji is burning your karma before your eyes. He is burning your karma in the ways that a spiritual master can do for another person. All of a sudden you start to feel lighter. You feel the burden lifted feeling that it is okay to be free and expand. You find yourself starting to feel happier, humble, and more grateful in the moment. To be forgiving and kind and loving. As you remember now your True Essence and you look at the bag of old karmas that is being burned for you now on the rim of the Grand Canyon.

Babaji says "Come with me, let me take you on your healing journey." As he touches your arm you turn and look at White Eagle as he nods and says "Yes it is time my child to go on your journey." As Babaji reaches over and touches your 3rd eye there is a great flash of light as you're standing facing the Grand Canyon. And as he steps out from the rim he starts to levitate as you start to levitate also. As he motions to you and says 'come.'

As you start to levitate out over the Canyon, now you are really feeling an even more expanded sense of the Canyon itself. You start to fly, you start to sail and hover forward and as you start to sail down into the Canyon, Babaji leads you through all of the rock formations as you're flying together, circling through walls and through great hidden valleys, rock formations, arches, great pillars of rock and stone.

And as you continue to fly deep deep down into the canyon, miles and miles down into the canyon. As you continue sailing all the way down Babaji is taking you all the way down, deep, deep down to the bottom of the Grand Canyon. And you can feel the energy shifting as you're sailing deeper and deeper into the Canyon. As you come closer you see a river.

Sailing faster and faster you're sailing right towards the river. Sailing deep, deep, deep down. Deep...deep...deep... down into the Mother Earth as you come splashing into the river. You now swim deep, deep down as you swim deeper and deeper continuing deeper. As you and Babaji continue to swim straight down you start to see a light up ahead in the distance ahead of you in the great deep. As you swim towards this light.

You find yourself coming into a great, great inner Cave of the Inner earth. A great secret, secluded and hidden cave. It's very large and spacious as you come down through a waterfall as you start to hover again as you're hovering in a great great inner world at the center of the great Mother Earth. It is pristine with mountains and trees.

There is a great central mountain with a great waterfall and crystal clear waters that are running down cascading down the rocks. And as you hear the water splashing and cascading trickling down and flowing down, you slowly and gently levitate down, down, down past all of the stages of the waterfall to the beautiful stream that the waterfall flows into.

And you land in front of the stream and as you go looking around there is so much to take in, so much beauty, so much peace and perfection and you just take a moment there with Babaji to be silent. As you continue to be silent and look down into the stream, and as he watches you he nods. As you continue to kneel down in front of the stream and you're looking at yourself in the water and you see that you have changed from the time you started this journey. You have become cleaner and clearer and lighter. You're being brought back into your True Self as you continue looking into the water.

Continuing to look deeper into your reflection you finally see your True Self and it gives you great joy. You feel great love and you feel the great love and the great peace in this place. As you now move your head and your face close to the water and you submerge the top part of your body and torso into the water you come out feeling completely clear, clean and refreshed in every way.

Taking the water and splashing it over your

head, face, neck and chest. You have come all this way to commune deep within the Mother Earth as she welcomes you here. Now as Babaji signals to you once again you both start to levitate as you both start to glide slowly up, up and away. Moving up past all of the stages of the waterfall again. As you glide sail and soar straight up towards the light at the top of the mountain.

As you now look down around the expansiveness of the Inner Earth with all of the trees and the beauty you feel now your own expansiveness. There are even animals here in this very quiet and peaceful divine place. There are also very larger crystal formations in certain areas that are beautifully shining with light and with energy. Beautiful tress and bushes, flowers and plants, heavily wooded, jungle like and pristine. As you float up towards the top of the mountain and you pass by it and up, up and away into the light. All the way up into the light. You find yourself coming up and out of the Grand Canyon as you start flying very quickly and as you are flying straight up towards the stars, the animal spirit familiars start to join you.

The spirit of Hawk, The spirit of Eagle, The spirit of Raven, the spirit of Dove, The spirit of Owl, the spirit of Jaguar, The spirit of Black Panther, The spirit of Tiger, The spirit of Lion, The spirit of Bear, The spirit of Deer, The spirit of Turtle, The spirit of Dolphin, and many, many other animal spirits come with you, and they gather around you and Babaji as you're flying together.

As you're both continuing to fly up towards the stars as you find yourself now out in the galaxy moving through the inner dimensions, moving beyond time and space. Moving in between the dimensions. As your flight has brought you here, the animal familiars will be gathering from among the stars and the celestial bodies the pieces of your Soul that have been lost in space.

The pieces or fragments of your Soul that have been lost in other dimensions, other realities, maybe even lost in the dream state. So as they fly with you every so often their flight pattern moves out away from you as they go after your Soul fragments. As you're doing a great, great circle around the Universe. So we allow for this journey beyond time and space in the Eternal Now. As the animal spirits are now gathering your Soul fragments and pieces...*pause for a moment*...

Babaji and You are now coming back around the Universe and back to the Milky Way, gathering Soul fragments the animal familiars continue as they are with you and Babaji. As you fly through the galaxy gathering, flying sailing and soaring. Coming back now towards the solar system that you know as home. Back across the planets of the solar system. And as you come to the Earth circling in you see the red pinpoints of light again all over the earth in many different places.

Where situations have happened in past lives and maybe even situations have happened in this life that may have taken more energy than was given. That had weighed heavy on your Soul in some way. Maybe an interaction or an instance where you lost a piece of yourself. You lost a part of who you are. And as you're flying with Babaji now over the oceans and over the continents as the red lights appear in each place the animal familiars swoop down and pick up the red light and as they pick up these red lights they turn them into gold.

The animals are bringing them all back. As you're now flying in a great field of gold with more of your energy returned to you. As now several orbits of the earth have been completed, you find yourself coming back down into the atmosphere to the Southwestern US as you're hovering straight down from the atmosphere. Hovering back down to North America, back to the Southwest, back to the Four Corners.

As you come down and you land on the Four Corners all of the animal spirits are flocking around you. And as you are now standing on the vortex point of the Four Corners. All of the animals are hovering around Babaji like a great halo and they are releasing to him this golden light, these soul pieces and as they are given to him in a great light he steps forward.

As he funnels his hands together and he bends down he blows all of your Soul energy back into your chest. (3 blowing sounds)

And as he does this your Soul is returning home to you. All of the golden light from all of your Soul fragments all of your lives among the stars, alternate realities, parallel universes, other places, other lifetimes here on planet earth and other moments and situations from this lifetime. All of these fragments were brought back to you as a great gift and blown back into your chest. Your energy is whole once again.

And with all of this new energy brought back to you be gentle with yourself over the next 48 hrs. Because now you have all of your Soul Power back. And you will notice that your emotions carry more energy. Emotions are energy in motion. Your thoughts feelings and your gestures carry more energy now. So people will respond to you as they feel more energy coming from you. So be gentle with yourself and others during this time as you are here in the circle.

As now White Eagle appears again from the ethers. and White Eagle thanks both of you and thanks Babaji as they bow to each other. Babaji then takes both of his hands as they start to glow calling down a Universal celestial blessing as he places both of his hands on your shoulders as he's grounding this energy into your body.

Grounding the Divine Celestial Energy of the Universe into your being. In a new way that will bring new wisdom and new insights for a new life. With a simple smile he bows his head to you as he steps back and becomes a great glow of energy. This glow of energy turns into a sphere once again, as the sphere floats now up, up and away. As it moves back up into the heavens and becomes very distant very quickly.

The sphere that was Babaji now becomes one of the star lights. One of the pin points, one of the stars again. White Eagle welcomes you back home and back into your body. He asks you now to sit down on the Four Corners, on the spirit of the North, South, East and West as the Great Mother Earth's vortex as these lay lines restore balance and ground your energy back into your body. Completely balanced on every level and grounded, completely healed and energized in every way. And as you sit here and receive this energy receive this blessing *...healing pause for a moment...*

We thank master Babaji Nagaraj and we thank White Eagle for both coming to participate on your behalf in this Akashic Shamanic Journey. May you go in peace, may you be well healed and whole again. In every way and every day, Namaste, Amen.

Chapter 11

PROTECTING AND CLEARING YOURSELF

*A*s we get into our spiritual studies and continue going deeper, at some point you are going to come in contact with the subject of clearing and protection if you haven't already. As we dive into our ever continuing adventures in energy we naturally become more sensitive to it. We are becoming more Self aware. As this occurs we tend to notice our good days and our bad days, our good moments and our bad moments a little more each time as we progress. Now the process of life itself and the spiritual path is supposed to get easier and more graceful or maybe this is what the ego would prefer looking through it's rose colored glasses. Life is really a sequence of events set up for our responses and learning as well as the ability to create and experience joy. According to our responses life may become more graceful or more challenging. It is really what we make of it. You've heard the saying 'If Life gives you lemons then make lemonade.'

As we become more sensitive on the spiritual path we naturally expect or envision our world to become more joyful and more graceful. When it isn't this creates conflict for us and we wonder what's going on? As we start to look around in search of answers, the central feeling is that we do not really feel comfortable within our place in our surroundings so we start to ask within and outside of ourselves as to what's going on.

As we are lead in the direction of spiritual cleansing, we start to see that there are procedures that need to be done when working with energy just as in the physical world, we must clean our houses, our bodies and our lives.

The need for cleansing can come from different reasons. If we are working in a place where there is a lot of dissonant energy or even just being in public where the energy is fast paced and stressful or maybe we have been around someone in business or personal interactions in which the exchange takes more energy than it gives.

Family as you may well know can be an ongoing source of confused interactions based on the past as well as preconceived notions about how everyone in the family should be acting. This is never easy for anyone and sometimes even more of a challenge when we start working with energy and start to see what's really going on behind the scenes. In this day and age it's usually that there is one person in particular in an immediate family that is the one who has awakened.

As this dynamic occurs the 'black sheep' or 'prodigal child' often is chastised by other family members for their beliefs or their lack of conformity. Family interactions can be even more tricky because the family is connected through the DNA where as friends or coworkers are not. This can require ancestral clearing which we talked about in Intermediate Vol. 2.

As we feel or participate in situations which are not pleasing or comfortable to us, we become aware of our needs to clear the exchange and sometimes to even protect ourselves.

Let's look at practical good old fashioned earthly ways to clear. If an unpleasant exchange takes place inside a building, often times breaking away to go for a walk will help to shift the energy. Getting out and walking freely and breathing deep can naturally do a lot for a person. Drinking plenty of water helps with feeling less stagnant especially if a person is prone to drink other types of drinks, coffee, soda, etc. Become more aware of your water intake and let it naturally clear your energy and your body.

Our bodies run on hydro-electric energy. Water, salt, oxygen, proteins and minerals. If you are getting an imbalance of other things such as caffeine, sugar, alcohol, to many carbohydrates, etc. then getting back to less or no junk food and good supplements backed by plenty of good water can be very helpful.

Exercise can clear stagnant energy from the body. Notice how you always feel a sense of accomplishment after getting something physically done.

Humor, comedy or laughter can really take the edge off of any uneasy situation or moment. Often when we have stress, tension or anxiety, anger, depression or sadness are involved. Getting some true laughter in your world can seriously interrupt all the over seriousness.

Forgiveness is one of the best natural 'cure-alls' in the world. It has the power to clear sickness or physical maladies from the body. Often when we have been carrying a heavy burden for too long we sometimes forget just how much it weighs on our bodies, minds and spirits. As we forgive ourselves and others, we can instantly become lighter, freer, happier and healthier. It is harder to be abundant when you may be carrying resentment for others or yourself. Remember that when Peter asked Jesus "How many times should I forgive my brother?" and Jesus said "Seven times, Peter". As Peter replied "Oh thank you, I understand now, seven times." Then Jesus again exclaimed" and then forgive him seventy times seven." (70 x 7) The reasoning behind this great statement is that all too often we may make a true attempt at forgiving something, someone or ourselves. As soon as we have let it go at another time we may find ourselves right back to carrying the burden and not understanding why it is there again and maybe even heavier. This is why it is called 'practicing forgiveness'. It's important to practice forgiving everything and everyone in a prayerful way. In this way we remember continually that we have forgiven or let the burden go, hopefully never to return.

Let's talk now about energy clearing. There are many ancient, traditional and newer ways of clearing energy from yourself, your space and your world.

The native Americans would use a **smudge stick** made of dried sage bundled together and tied with a special colored string while they are saying prayers and blessings. This is common to find in spiritual shops or even online. The sage is lit with fire until it smolders producing a thick smoke which is then waved through your energy fields either by yourself or another person. As you do this you may say a prayer statement such as:

"I clear myself now of any negative and/or disharmonic energies and fill myself up with peace, love, joy, harmony and abundance. "

You may find the smudging process online or have someone show you how to do it. This clears the airspace of unwanted spirits and elemental energies that may be built up or lingering over time.

I have also found many gemstones or types of crystals to be very effective in clearing a persons energy as well as protecting them against negative outside influences. Selenite is one of the best universal clearing stones because it's actually a form of petrified salt. Selenite is also self clearing so as you use it either with yourself or others it continually clears itself. For this reason it's used by many healers. Black Tourmaline is very protective and clearing for us and for electronic devices such as computers. Black Obsidian, Jade, Amethyst, and Rose Quartz are just a few of the minerals that can be very supportive and protective for you. You will learn which ones work best as you experiment with them.

Taking Salt baths can be a very good source of clearing. Getting into the ocean if you have access to it can also help because of it's natural salt content. Exercising, running, walking and swimming are all very good ways to move the energy in the body.

Doing a periodic dietary cleanse of the body is very important. Cleansing the colon of debris and parasites is always important. This can clear you energetically in ways you never thought possible while allowing you to reach new heightened levels of clarity. Parasite and viruses seem to have their own consciousness and they want to move in, take over and feed. Through the gut as we use our guts to think, feel and process, these little critters get a hold and start telling the gut to tell us that they want more sugar and more junk. Using a good probiotic daily can be very important. Please consult a dietician or another practitioner or investigate trusted sources of information as you start cleansing. This way you know what to expect.

Many sources of negative energy are usually linked to certain things in the body, though they may appear to be etheric in nature. So there are many angles, methods and approaches we can take to healing, clearing and protecting. The main first step is becoming aware of the need to clear and protect. The next step is engaging in the process. The third element is to continue the process through to finish and create a schedule of intention for future cleanses.

Often times we may get a clearing and feel much better afterwards and think that it's all over, everything is done. While in the moment this is true, we want to make sure and keep ourselves clear and protected from time to time. Knowing that you need it and not taking action does not solve the problem or keep you clear. So take action.

There are many different types of elemental

energies, alien energies, disembodied people in limbo, and even dark or demonic energies that are out there. They are all seeking expression here on the earth plane as well as other dimensions. Over the course of doing my work I have had some 'run ins' and 'show downs' with strange beings and energies.

Working from the Light with compassion is always the best place to come from. Working from the ego as if you're involved in an action thriller movie could get you in more trouble than you bargain for, because you are lowering your vibration in order to engage these spirits in a drama or showdown. Remember, they have vast resources just like the Light beings, so be careful.

The best place to always come from is going to be Love. When you are coming from a continual place of Love anything and everything that is operating at lower levels of energy cannot attach or bother you if you are in a place of Love. You can acknowledge them and they can acknowledge you but their is no alignment between the vibrations unless you lower your vibration and allow it.

Sometimes things happen so don't judge yourself too harshly. It is possible to start vibrating with fear or anger and allow something in because it can attach to lower frequencies. Understanding this will help you to focus on keeping your vibration high and in so doing also clear. Love is the best answer to everything. Got aliens? Show them the Love. Got demons? Show them the Love. Neither of those groups can do anything to you or with you as long as you are in pure Love. Practice Love, Gratitude and Forgiveness.

The main thing to know with this work of accessing the Akashic Records is that their aren't any ways that dark energies or beings can get to you through the Records. It just won't happen. If you have been working in other places, realms or with other beings and your energy is off then you definitely want to start clearing and protecting yourself. This will help you to have clearer experiences as you continue to practice your skills of Accessing the Akashic Records.

Practice Daily:

Practice Loving the world around you and
Everyone you come in contact with.

Practice Gratitude for everything you
Have in your life and
Everything that you've been through.

Practice Forgiveness with Everyone
In your life that has wronged you
Or that you have wronged.

Most of All
Love Yourself, Forgive Yourself,
Thank Yourself, and Be Kind to Yourself

Exercise 3

JOURNEY TO ANCIENT ATLANTIS

*A*s we prepare to journey to Ancient Atlantis, Take a few moments to get yourself comfortable in the very best way possible for you. There are other scripts that we have guided you through to relax all parts of the body, utilize this protocol now. Sitting in a reclined position or laying down will be the best positions for you. A light blanket to cover the body to make it feel supported and safe is always helpful. Taking in now some long slow deep breaths and allowing every part of your body to relax.

Continually relaxing deeper and deeper moment by moment, feeling perfect relaxation filling your body. Now that you've done your intro meditation and you've relaxed down, down, down even deeper, you are ready.

You find yourself walking along a path now and focusing the mind on the exercise of walking. As you're relaxing and walking now you are thinking of the ocean. And the next thing you know in the next moment you are transported their and walking along some beautiful cliffs beside the ocean. These cliffs mark a continent and edge of a great plateau. As you now look out across the ocean you can smell the ocean mist. You keep on walking alongside the cliffs and between huge rocks jetting straight up from the beach and towering over head as the water from the ocean mist and surf slashes close to you every so often.

It's the perfect temperature and it's the perfect day. It seems as though you could look down the coastline into forever. So now as you look down this coastline into forever you continue walking wondering what's up ahead and just around the next turn. As you continue walking and you look off to your left you see a pathway that's leading up the side of the hill up through the foothills and through a mountainous terrain.

It looks as though this remote path has been traveled before and is easy to gain your footing, so as you decide to do it and you take the first steps, you start to climb very steadily with strength exerting your legs, muscles and body. You feel good about this climb.

As you keep winding up the path and you look up now along this mountainous wall of rock you are climbing through, as you're climbing up this cliff which seems very steep and yet easy to foot as you take great exhilarating strides as you walk straight up this slightly winding path.

Continuing straight up you see the sun up overhead now. As you look out from below you notice that you're starting to move away from the ocean and the beach. As you're looking out now across the great ocean and the beach, you start to expand your awareness and you feel as if you are becoming taller or expanding.

As you look ahead up into the sun you feel as though your mind is expanding up to reach and to touch into the sun. And as you look down you feel your feet expanding deep within the side of the cliff and deep within the rocks below you can feel a great expansive connection all the way down to the beach.

This makes you feel as though you are expanding in both directions and growing taller. Your awareness is expanded now. As you continue to climb up this cliff, up, up and away, winding and headed towards the sun straight up the hill. Finally you reach the top and you are walking along now and come to stand on the flat of the earth of this higher plateau. As you walk now across the earth you feel so expanded. You feel yourself merge with the sun again and merge with the earth again.

You feel like your head is in the sun and your feet are deep, deep within the earth. As this happens it expands your consciousness and your awareness.

Walking along you now come to a sacred site here on this plateau overlooking the ocean. You have come to a sacred garden where there are some very large sacred amethyst geodes that are standing in a great half circle before you.

There are 7 geodes. And as you connect with these geodes you realize that they are portals of earth wisdom and knowledge. There is a deep void within each amethyst geode as they stand before you like great hooded figures. Great wisdom keepers they are. Each one of them has a slightly different vibration as they all tell a story together and they all have their own stories to tell.

As you stand before them you start to look into each one.

The first amethyst says:

"I am the knowledge and wisdom of time."

The second amethyst says:

"I am the knowledge and wisdom of space."

The third amethyst says:

"I am the knowledge and wisdom of light."

The fourth amethyst says:

"I am the knowledge and wisdom of color."

The fifth amethyst says:

"I am the knowledge and wisdom of sound."

The sixth amethyst says:

"I am the knowledge and wisdom of void and
   depth."
The seventh amethyst says:
"I am the knowledge and wisdom of the All."

As they are all here telling a story and talking to
you. You now look deep within each geode you find
your consciousness tending towards the one that is
drawing you the most, you take that passageway as
you move towards the geode. Connecting deep, deep
down within the earth. As you move towards the
geode and you connect deep, deep down within
the earth. You start to move into the geode and you
merge with the geode. You find yourself traveling
as they are all connected together. You're traveling
deep, deep down within the earth to a deep place of
knowledge and wisdom within the earth traveling
deep, traveling down, down, down. As you travel
now down within the earth now expanding you
come to a very large great hall. The Great Halls of
Amenti.

The Seven amethyst geodes have led you to this
great circular hall deep within the earth. In this
circular hall there are 7 doorways and 7 directions
and there is an 8th direction. Each doorway and
direction is associated with each geode. Time,
space, light, color, sound, void or depth of All
the All of Omnipresence and the 8th doorway
represents Soul.

As you stand there you now are welcomed by the sound of a great voice seeming to come from all around you. "Welcome to the Great Halls of Amenti dear Soul." The voice is very deep and strong though has a very gentle nature. In a great flash of light a very tall man appears before you know. About 7 feet tall with dark hair. He is wearing a rainbow colored head dress and is very healthy and strong in appearance.

"I Am Thoth the Atlantean. I have come to meet you here to acknowledge your bravery in stepping forth on your path of Self Discovery and Knowing. My energy is radiant in All ways as I have walked the Ancient path of Self Exploration in Atlantis and discovered the keys to all of the great doors before you."

"I have come to understand love, light, sound, color and knowledge as true wisdom. You may ask any question or think any thought at this time and here in the radiance of true wisdom you will receive direct answers and direct knowing. Take a few moments here and now to ask questions that may be of immediate concern to you. Ponder the thoughts and questions that you would like to receive advice and help with." *...pause for a few moments...*

As you meditated and received trustworthy insights and messages from within your own thoughts you are now understanding new ways of creatively receiving insights. Thoth now offers healing and clearing energy for you in a new and unique way.

"I will project my energy as the strength of my radiance will light your energy vibration. Anything that you wish to release or discover hidden within yourself will now come to the Light. My energy is bright, strong and steadfast much like that of Arc Angel Metatron, though I ascended from human. I taught myself ascension by studying the Hermetic laws of the Universe including Love and Forgiveness above all things. Receive now healing and clearing as my energy levels expand to increase your vibration. This will take a few moments so relax and receive."

...You can feel the upgrades and activations taking place in your energy fields. You can feel the heightened awareness and vibrations that you're now experiencing as total clarity.

Thoth now says "My spirit will go with you on this journey. I will become invisible and remain silent as a guide in order for you to receive the best insights through your own Soul."

So as you now turn to these doorways as you look into each one they expand you in both ancient and new unique ways. And as you continue to look into them and you feel into them you feel yourself starting to merge with the doorways that are pulling you the most in a certain direction of the circular hall.

And as you travel there through the doorway of Time and Space traveling through the stars, you feel like great distances have been traveled in the blink of an eye. In the next moment you find yourself in an amazing place. In a great and ancient civilization full of islands with temples and statues. And great virtuous pieces of art in this place that you have traveled to from deep within the earth from the Hall of Amenti.

Through the doorway of time and space you have traveled to ancient Atlantis. And as you are here in Atlantis now you are looking and touching and feeling and sensing everything around you. The buildings and the great halls as you're touching the walls and feeling the stone they are made from.

Touching the sculptures and feeling the texture of the marble from which they were carved. Feeling and sensing now the great craftsmanship that went into making all of the great works of art and the murals and paintings that stand before you of the buildings and halls, temples and walls.

In this ancient time and in this ancient Atlantean city, your consciousness has been expanded, your senses expand out as you are now experiencing 360 degree circular vision or even spherical vision. You can see, feel and sense everything in a circular pattern or in a sphere pattern around. Continually in every direction at the same time. Above, below, to each side and behind. Wherever you think or direct your mind, you sense, feel and see into that direction on all levels.

Deeply connected with all things and all people while visiting this place you are in total sync with the inhabitants of Atlantis. During this time everyone is experiencing this dynamic of expanded awareness. As it expands out it activates both sides of the brain. In a very heightened way of awareness. It activates and adds to your mental capacity in every way super-charging your mind and your senses.

You use your eyes and your 3rd eye to look directly ahead to focus on life in front of you and yet whenever you choose to, you expand and you look out in every direction simultaneously, instantly and continuously connected with all things at all times.

This is the ancient Atlantean Way. So as you use your senses to navigate the way with whatever is in front of you, your senses move in a spherical pattern all around you continually. Your energy sphere connects deeply with the world around you in every way. And as your energy field connects out as your senses, your energy field and your mind field.

Your chakra fields and your Soul field connects out in every direction around you. This is the ancient Atlantean Way. And as your fields collaborate and intermingle with nature and your surroundings you realize that there is an incredible power and potential for manifesting as you are completely continually connected with your surroundings in an energetic way as are other people in this place, experiencing the same ways and also with each other. It is a very sensual experience. It is a very expanded and heightened experience involving all of your senses deeply connected and experiencing your surroundings in this place at all times in 360 degrees. As your senses are also able to focus continually on the Here and Now in front of you.

Expanding out and radiating out in this spherical pattern connecting you with your surroundings here in Atlantis. And as this energy of perception continues to radiate out around your presence, you are now walking through the villages and through the city. You come to the center of the city of the village and you see what looks to be a great light source in front of you.

And this great light source is comprised of plants and trees and crystals of the Earth. These plants and trees and crystals of the Earth are interwoven together in front of you in unique patterns. As the energy of the plants, trees and crystals are all interwoven together, they create great patterns of organic light messaging. And now the closer you study this you can feel a deep, deep connection with the plants.....and a deep,

deep connection with the trees....and a deep, deep connection with the crystals. You can feel that they are all alive, interwoven and intertwined. As you feel the energy impulses here, you look into these intertwined patterns and you see messages and symbols and even mandalas of light. So amazing is this ancient Earth time, place and space and organic energy technology.

The Atlanteans called this the Selfic. The Selfic energy of Earth and Light. Completely organic, naturally of the Earth and so completely alive. It speaks volumes naturally and continually. Singing with energy. These energy patterns move out in every direction as it moves through your sensual field. As it moves through your field in this spherical awareness. It moves out in every way out across time and space amplifying the oneness that you feel with all of the world, nature and all of time and space as it moves out across the ancient land of Atlantis.

As it connects deeply energetically, mentally and inter-dimensionally with you as you time travel and bi-locate into each of seven sacred temples. Seven sacred underground chambers.

A great temple of Light and Color. A great temple of Time and Space. A great temple of Sound. A great temple of Void of depth. A great temple of the Soul. A great temple of Love. And A great hidden temple of the All. And at this time allow your mind, your rainbow fields, your chakras, your energy to move out and connect with each one of these Sacred Halls. Receiving the gifts of energy activations. Receiving natural and heightened organic Awareness and Integration, Receiving Healing and Love. Any messages that may come to you naturally as being an ancient Atlantean citizen. You may naturally receive these now. Though if you were not an Ancient Atlantean citizen you are still able to benefit completely and participate fully as we are all connected. Through these natural powerful completely organic ways with the original Earth and the originating reality of the Earth.

So as you now move your Body, Mind and Soul through each one of these original sacred temples. (*pause for a few moments in each Temple*)

Through now the Temples of Time and the cycles
  of Time, and Space...
Through now the Temple of Light and Color...
Through now the Temple of Sound...
Through now the Temple of Depth and Void...
Through now the Temple of Love...
Through now the Temple of Soul...
Through now the Temple of the All.

Traveling deep within each temple and receiving gifts of wisdom, understanding and activation.

As you now have spent some quality time here in observation today on this journey of connecting with Ancient Atlantis and the true nature of the Divinity, and the organic original earth reality dimension and it's gifts that has been given in the expansion of your awareness and your senses and your energy in every way. With your spherical awareness as you are moving through the different temples. From whichever temple you now are standing in to radiate out your great spherical awareness to encompass all of the other sacred temples.

And a great love and a great gratitude to all of the people all of the Souls all of the earth all of the civilization as you start to merge back through the temple of time and space you merge back through a portal to the Great Halls of Amenti. As you're now standing in the circular hall once again deep within the Earth and their are seven doorways around you and you can feel the energy coming through each doorway and then it goes out in a different direction across the universe for a different purpose and yet they are all connected and intersected.

Now as you look straight up through a great dome that offers you again circular spherical vision and senses you see the sun and the sun is calling you through this portal of light and as you focus on the sun your feet become light as it starts to draw you up, up and away, moving up as it continues to draw you up, and as you come up feeling lighter, regenerated and super charged you come back up to the surface to the great plateau overlooking the ocean. Again you find yourself standing there before the seven great earth elders as the giant amethyst geodes.

And as you look into each one you say a prayer of thankfulness, almost as if you are asking each one in amazement "How could you have known?" They are All so connected and all so continually aware in all of the inter-dimensional times, places and spaces and the temples are all connected deeply in every way. It gives you a great working model and a great sense of oneness. A new sense of oneness that you can use from now on in a new way. With your energy fields your spherical senses and your energy vision. This is also linked directly to the visions and energy that are before you that guide and direct you through linear time past present and future before you. So you are part of the continual time scape and event horizon past,present and future with your mind, your senses and your vision laid out before you and within you as well as the great spherical senses in all directions.

As you move out across time and space, you are now able to influence matter and potentials locally around you. The dreams, the visions and everything that you have sought to manifest is within these fields, pure potentiality, around your body and your body is also connected deeply and directly with these spherical fields with the original template of the original Earth Spirit. And She has the great, great power to manifest for you and with you in great ways. And so now enjoy working with the energy of Ancient Atlantis and the true nature of the energy, the people and the time, place and space. We thank the 7 elders and Thoth the Atlantean for their assistance and we bow to you All.

Om, Peace, Amen.

Exercise 4

MEETING MERLIN WITHIN THE AKASHIC RECORDS

*A*s we prepare to journey to ancient Atlantis, Take a few moments to get yourself comfortable in the very best way possible for you. There are other scripts that we have guided you through to relax all parts of the body. Sitting in a reclined position or laying down will be the best positions for you. A light blanket to cover the body to make it feel supported and safe is always helpful. Taking in now some long slow deep breaths and allowing every part of your body to relax.

Continually relaxing deeper and deeper moment

by moment, feeling perfect relaxation filling your body. As you now find yourself looking up to the sky and standing outside in nature. As you look up into the depths of the sky you see the perfect light of the cosmos and a pin point opening above you that is a direct passage to the Divine Source of All Creation.

This Light comes down and showers you, as it comes down now just for You. As it comes down it is spiraling down in a great motion all around you. As it is churning and turning and spiraling down now through your crown and through every part of your body. Down through your crown, through your 3rd eye and down through your head and brain, your face and your senses.

The Light is spiraling now down through your throat chakra and neck, through your shoulders and chest, your heart chakra. Down through your arms and hands. Through your fingers and spiraling out your fingers this light emanates from your hands.

This Universal Divine Source Light of God is coming in and clearing everything out and releasing everything that is ready to go. It is also clearing everything out that is not of your origins or for your highest good. Filling you with Light, spiralling down through your heart, lungs and all of your organs in your mid section. Down through your back and your stomach. Through your Solar plexus chakra, sacral chakra and your base chakra. Down through your hips, your spine, your tailbone and pelvis as the light now spirals down through each leg. Down through your thighs and knees. The light is spiraling down through your calves and your shins clearing any and all negativity that's not of your making. Anything and everything that is meant to release and clear at this time leaves you now as it moves down and out through your feet. Deep down into the Earth where it's recycled into pure positive energy.

And as the Light continues to spiral down around you it now creates the perfect portal. This perfect White Light fills your consciousness, fills your fields. and your heart, mind, body and Soul. As the Light starts to now soften creating a great field of white and gold around you, find yourself now looking through the portal of Light out into what seems to be an ancient study. A personal library or study chamber. There are very many unique objects and crystals lining the room. Energy tools for alchemy, astronomy and science. Tools for studying the stars and the ocean through maps. As many ancient books line the walls of this ancient study. As you're panning your vision around this study you find it to be very peaceful yet energetic in a spiritual nature.

As you turn to your left you now see a great hallway. There are candles lining the hall and at the end of the hall is a great door. The door opens now very slowly revealing a great White Light that shines from the other side from beyond through the door. A figure, a silhouette now steps through the door. As this figure, this silhouette comes closer and starts to step out of the Light, out of the doorway casting a show into the hallway. As the door now slowly closes. And the light from the candles in the hallway now continues to grow bright. As the figure comes closer, we now get a sense that this is the keeper of this study. A man in medium build and height, stately, slow moving, graceful. This figure with long hair and a long beard wearing a multi colored robe trimmed in green and gold. He is carrying a great staff. And as silent as this man is, there seems to be a great amount of energy he is carrying with him.

As he comes out into the room to greet you. As he comes closer you start to see his features. Long white hair and a long white beard with some color. A large strong frame of a man. And with a gentle smile He greets you. He says "Welcome to my study, my name is Merlin, and I have been awaiting your arrival. I'm sure that you have many questions, so we will have a discussion to meet your curiosities and inspire your imagination and your intuition to greater depths and to higher levels."

So as Merlin walks around the study he shows you the books and the crystals and the star maps, oceanic maps and alchemical tools that he has used for centuries. As he now perches himself on a tall stool, with one leg up he rests his arm on a counter top holding his staff. He now welcomes you to sit down across from him. So as you do now sit down, Merlin starts to tell a story. He invites you to connect with him here in a silent meditation for a few moments.

As you are now connecting with Merlin here directly in meditation, this is a great gift he is giving you. His energy is honoring your great mind in a wonderful way. His energy is heightening your awareness and it's also bringing an awareness and a deep peace to your mind. To know that you are in the graces and the presence of a kindred spirit. Someone who understands you. Someone who has done the work over and over many times over and stood where you are on the path of curiosity and self study. So this meeting of the minds with the great Merlin is a serendipitous gift, you might say from the Universe. As Merlin's energy is inspiring to You, it is opening your consciousness and your mind.

As he says mentally to you "There are many things that I can show you." So as Merlin opens his eyes and he connects with you, he wants to tell you a story.

"Dear One come with me and I will show you, I will tell you of my past and my path. The name 'Merlin' is only a representation. The name 'Merlin' is symbolic of the blackbird, the Raven. The name 'Merlin' is symbolic of a tool or a hammer. The name 'Merlin' is symbolic of a teacher. The name 'Merlin' is symbolic of a messenger. So it is a nick name or a designation more so than anything else. And as I have been called many things in my past, one thing is for sure, I was a warrior and a leader of kings. I used my creativity and my intuition wisely to guide the destiny of mankind in ancient Europe. To name and christen kings and kingdoms. There were many great movements in history that I was part of. My intuition was so profound that it was often times referred to as magic. There was a great destiny of Arthur and his knights of the round table as there was a great destiny for the kingdom of Camelot. To balance and reorganize or reinvent the destiny of the ancient Celtic regions of Europe that was wrought with confusion. With many nomadic tribes there was no easy way, but in the days through decision, intuition and stealth cleared a way. So you see the name Merlin was more of a nickname than anything else. "

"Also in these ancient times it was considered blasphemous to call someone by their true name. In the early days, in the early ages, All of the great leaders, kings and priests, had sur names. And those who were of royal descent. So it was deemed unlawful, rude and impolite to call someone or address them by their true name. It is the same as today pointing your finger at someone. As it is a projection of energy so to speak. So it was thought that someone would take someone else's energy or bind them through magic."

"This can be likened in your current modern world to be the same as talking about someone you are placing their energy into a stasis, a binding, a tether through time and conversation. This is why the ancient masters have said that it is better never to gossip about another person. Never to talk or to tell stories of another. Although sometimes we do in order to teach and to understand and learn. So we walk the middle ground, the middle path, As I in my own history, have had to walk the middle ground as a great warrior and a leader."

"My energy is of the Dragon and the Dragon is magic. Dragons are mystical creatures created of magic and very rare. I am of White Dragon energy. This is not to be confused with reptilian energy in any way. The dragon energy is sacred. And the sacred holy fire of the Light from which the Dragon emanates is the Christ Light Coming down once again through these later ancient times. In my later years I was naturally and intuitively channelling the original Christ teachings once again from another lifetime of having walked with the master. These messages, insights and magical healing energy that emanated from me came through from being in the original presence of Master Jesus the Holy Spirit and the Apostles."

"As I have created the dragon, the dragon has also created me. We are one, we stand as one. I am he and he is me. Timeless, immortal, the white dragon is one of many. There are many colors of dragons, and each color of dragon represents a different color aspect or nature of the Universal. All in balance. The White,

Blue, Red, Green, Violet, Black and Golden Dragons all represent a balance in the mystical nature of the Universe. A balance of power within the 7 different Dragons.

So as Merlin now stands, and taps his staff 3 times on the floor as the great crystal atop the staff activates with Earth magic. As he holds his staff high in the air. It seems he is calling or conjuring a portal of light. As the crystal atop his staff begins to glow with spiritual energy, and he looks you in the eyes, he then turns his gaze straight up to the heavens as you see now a great portal of light opening through the transparent holographic ceiling of the study, far up in the heavens. As he brings his great staff down swiftly and grounds it on the floor, sparks fly out in a great flurry.

At this time there is a great portal of light opening again from above. As the light comes spiraling down once again there is a great white being coming down through the light in spiral patterns as this light shines down all around you. It is a great white Dragon, spiraling slowly, descending down through great spirals. As you see the unique nature and the grand nature of the white dragon, coming closer you can see how huge the Dragon is. Towering 10-12 feet tall as the dragon flies down and lands behind Merlin in the holographic study. And as you're looking now at the white Dragon and looking at Merlin, they are both looking back at you. It is a great energy to be in the presence of them both and to behold this moment.

And so now Merlin says "So now you see, the White Dragon is me and I am he. You now understand the great nature of the presence of the dragon. As the Dragon looks at you there is a fierce presence and yet a subtle calmness. There are sparks of energy everywhere around them, magic energy that are coming from the Dragon itself as it also emanates a great field of energy. As you now understand this presence, this oneness and symbiotic relationship between them. The white Dragon symbolizes and embodies the powerful spiritual magic of the Light of the good. God's magic.

"That I have been known for in folklore through the ages and centuries. And now it is true as I have ascended and I am now part of God's magic. For you see, I am he and the white dragon is me." And as you stand beholding their presence, moving back to the beginning.

So now Merlin says "Come and let me show you Great Halls of Wisdom. Let us go on a journey together. And as he motions to you the Dragon turns around and Merlin starts to walk up the back of the Dragon. And he motions you to come with him. So as you walk also up the back of the Dragon you both now climb and sit atop the shoulders. As now the Dragon's wings start to move. You can feel the great momentum of the wings, though you know that the dragon and it's body are also moving by magic, God's magic. As he starts to levitate up and float and all 3 of you move up in great spirals of light. Moving up out of the holographic study of Merlin's library. Moving straight up. Up, up and away through the night sky and all of the stars.

Through these great spirals up through the portal of Light. And as you come up through the great clouds you come up through and into a great castle, into a great temple, a great hall. Coming down off the back of the Dragon you and Merlin both stand now in the great hall. As you purvey the inside of the great hall you notice family crests or coats of arms hanging all the way around the top of the walls in this great castle. All the way around the top of this hall. As you view the hall and you look now at the dragon, Merlin says "Welcome to the great Hall of Records. Your intuition and your Soul has brought you here. Welcome home to the Akashic Records."

As you're looking around in this expanded state in this heightened awareness in this peaceful place, Merlin now stretches his arms out wide and as he lifts his hands now. The white dragon now takes a long slow deep breathe and he blows out white fire. A white spiritual fire. This white spiritual fire cleanses and fills up the whole inside of this hall. It moves though your body, your aura, your fields and through your mind, cleansing you, healing, protecting, balancing and energizing. Cleansing you, healing protecting, balancing and energizing you. And as Merlin witnesses you here in this space and the realm of the Akashic Hall of Records, here in this mystical place.

He says to you "Dear One, please take a moment and search the queries of your mind and your Soul. What is the question at this time that your heart desires the answer to? What curious mystery of yourself would you like to have solved?"

And as Merlin asks you this and you're looking into his eyes. The answer to the question starts to form. Just as you start to ask this question, the Dragon connecting with Merlin takes a deep breath and the dragon blows out fire again right in front of you.

And in this bright spiritual fire there are very bright light Akashic symbols that are breathing and moving with energy. And they hover in front of you as you now feel and sense the story of these symbols and the messages that they hold.

Just take a few moments to look into this vision deeper as the thoughts, feelings and ideas emerge from deep within you here in the Akashic Records. As you now sense the creativity and the knowledge and wisdom that is contained within these dancing symbols of light.

Now Merlin asks you once again "Dear One, what messages, knowledge or wisdom would you like to receive from your queries here deep within the Akashic Hall of Wisdom? What may we answer for you from the depths of your Soul?"

As you connect and you're looking through Merlin's eyes, he knows what your question is even before you do. And as the question starts to come from your heart, mind, body and Soul Merlin signals the dragon once more, and the Dragon takes a deep breath with white fire in his eyes, he breaths out that white fire again before you as the Akashic symbols appear once again in the spiritual fire in the air before you. These spiritual symbols create answers to your questions deep from within your Soul. And as you study the symbols and their moving light energy. They bring a special knowing to you that comes directly into your mind, body heart and your Soul.

Once more Merlin speaks and says "Dear One, let us show you your Soul Directory. Let us show you your lifetimes through this Divine Directory of your Soul. And as he taps his staff on the floor of the Great Temple of Wisdom once more 3 times very gently and the Great White Dragon takes a deep breath.

Taking in the essence of the Hall of Wisdom and blows out a great spiritual light, a great spiritual fire which once again is host to a great collection of light symbols coming out of the ethers and dancing all through your chakras energy fields and your Soul field. All of these symbols are direct soul symbols of each lifetime that you have lived. Like the great family crests that are adorning the top of the walls in this great Hall.

So take a few moments no to study these Soul Symbols and you may even go into one, two or a few of these symbols and look at that essence of You, that part of You or that lifetime. Just take a few moments in silence as Merlin and the Dragon will be here in your presence holding space for you.

And now as you are looking at all of these Soul Symbols and the integrations that you have received from each lifetime. Merlin says you are welcome to come back here to travel to the Great Hall and to sit in meditation to visualize. To see, to listen to watch the visions and to remember as you look into each lifetime here in the Great Hall of Wisdom.

At this time Merlin says, "Dear One, I here the earth is calling you home. Your body and your life is calling you home. So let us take you back now." As Merlin motions to you again to climb onto the back of the Great White Dragon. As the dragon now lets out one final breath of Divine Spiritual Fire as a blessing to this castle and this Great Hall.

As you are leaving you view once more the family crests hanging all around the great castle walls. These are all of your different lifetimes being shown to you here within the Records. And you will connect back here when you come to study each of these lifetimes for your personal Self Knowing and Discovery.

Now as the great castle door and draw bridge is

lowered at the entry of the Great Hall. The Dragon with you and Merlin on his shoulders starts to fly out through this great opening. Across the clouds through space and then straight down through the clouds. Coming out of the clouds now you are all spiraling down as the earth is coming closer. And you can feel the great spiritual energy, and the great thought and caring that went into creating this spiritual voyage for you.

As you continue to spiral down, all 3 of you together spiraling down, down, down to Earth. As the Earth comes closer and closer. The Great Being Mother Earth and her energy is calling you home. Now you are returning back down through the clouds of the atmosphere. Back to your continent in this lifetime and to the area in which you live.

And Merlins says now "It is time to bring you back, and to part ways for the time being, but take heed my friend we will be watching, and we will be here for you, and we will come forth again when we are called by You with noble intention and when the time is right. You can call us from within the Akashic Records and we will be there with you once again. "

As you all fly down closer to your home, Merlin holds up his staff as he looks over his shoulder at you, your hair blowing in the wind. As the crystal atop Merlin's staff glows with a very powerful orb of light. This orb of light increases and grows brighter and brighter so that the orb surrounds you now. The soft energy of this great orb of Light transports you back down and grounding into your body instantly. Back into your world and your home. With soothing, healing and super activating energy as a great blessing. As you see Merlin and the great Dragon you moving back into the higher dimensions from whence they came. Always present in the waves of the higher ethers and always ready to work with you. We thank you Merlin and the great White Dragon. We thank the Keepers of the Records and the Great Akashic Hall of Wisdom for all of the great spiritual truths and wisdoms today and we look forward to your return once again.

Om, Peace, Amen

Exercise 5

JOURNEY
TO THE
AKASHIC
RECORDS
OF THE
SUN

$\mathcal{A}$s we now prepare to Journey to the Akashic Records of the Sun, take a few moments to get yourself comfortable in the very best way possible for you. Sitting in a reclined position or laying down will be the best positions for you. A light blanket to cover the body to make it feel supported and safe is always helpful. Taking in now some long slow deep breaths and allowing every part of your body to relax.

Continually relaxing deeper and deeper moment by moment, feeling perfect relaxation filling your body.

We start the relaxation process and the journey process for the journey into the Sun by doing the alternate nostril breathing process, Nadi Shodhana (*found in Vol. 2 and the workbook*) followed by a vocal toning for each of the chakras to open and utilizing the Uttarabodhi mudra with each chakra. (*the yogic hand gesture for enlightenment*)

Uttarabodhi Mudra - The fingers interlock, leaving the index fingers and thumbs extended. The tips of the index fingers touch, pointing upward, and the tips of the thumbs touch as well, pointing downward.

Utilize now the Uttarabodhi mudra pointing the thumbs at the base chakra close to the groin area. As you now chant in the key of C these sanscrit seed syllables from ancient Indian tantric (*technique*) spiritual practice for opening each chakra.

Chanting in the key of C and focusing on the color ruby red for the base chakra...

LAH, BAH, RAH, YAM, HAH, AHA, AUM

Move the hands now in the Uttarabodhi mudra pointing the thumbs at the sacral chakra in the lower stomach belly button area.

Chanting in the key of D and focusing on the color bright orange for the sacral chakra...

LAH, BAH, RAH, YAM, HAH, AHA, AUM

Move the hands now in the Uttarabodhi mudra pointing the thumbs at the solar plexus chakra in the lower stomach area.

Chanting in the key of E and focusing on the color bright yellow for the solar plexus chakra...

LAH, BAH, RAH, YAM, HAH, AHA, AUM

Move the hands now in the Uttarabodhi mudra pointing the thumbs at the heart chakra in the center of your chest.

Chanting in the key of F and focusing on the color bright green for the heart chakra...

LAH, BAH, RAH, YAM, HAH, AHA, AUM

Move the hands now in the Uttarabodhi mudra pointing the thumbs at the throat chakra in the center of your chest.

Chanting in the key of G and focusing on the color

bright blue for the throat chakra...
LAH, BAH, RAH, YAM, HAH, AHA, AUM

Move the hands now in the Uttarabodhi mudra pointing the thumbs at the 3rd eye chakra in the center of your chest.

Chanting in the key of A and focusing on the color royal blue or indigo for the 3rd eye chakra...
LAH, BAH, RAH, YAM, HAH, AHA, AUM

Move the hands now in the Uttarabodhi mudra pointing the thumbs at the crown chakra over the top of your head. Chanting in the alternate keys of B and D and focusing on the color violet for the crown chakra...
LAH, BAH, RAH, YAM, HAH, AHA, AUM

As we are preparing the chakras and the kundalini energy for this journey into the sun to meet the solar angels and deities. As you relax now getting comfortable and continue your long slow breathing. Now that we have activated all of the chakras,

Your base chakra is glowing with a beautiful bright Red.

Your sacral chakra is glowing with a beautiful bright Orange.

Your solar plexus chakra is glowing with a beautiful bright Yellow.

Your heart chakra is glowing with a beautiful bright Green.

Your throat chakra is glowing with a beautiful
  bright Blue.
Your crown chakra is glowing with a beautiful
  Violet and rainbow colors.

As you are now aware that all of your chakras
are glowing very brightly and spinning in balance.
Right over your solar plexus there is a great
rainbow ball of light that is growing. Bright as
the sun, giving rainbow light as it continues to
grow brighter and brighter. As this ball of energy
moves out across the home and property and the
surroundings of where you are relaxing now.

As this light, your light, continues expanding out
encompassing the whole town or region in which
you live. Continuing to expand until it engulfs the
whole country in which you live and then finally
the whole continent on which you live. As you
expand this light, your light is overtaking the oceans
and every continent. Scandinavia, The UK, Europe,
North America, South America, the Middle East,
the Far East, Asia, Russia, and Australia. Until you
notice the whole world is shining very brightly in
your light.

As the whole world is now shining very brightly
in your light you may have noticed that you have
ascended up over the planet. As you are here in space
looking down at the beautiful Earth turning ever so
slowly, you start to notice red pin points of light on
some of the continents. Some are closer together,

some are farther apart. Just take a few moments to locate and view these pin point of light. These are your past lives here on planet earth.

As you're floating here in the upper outer atmosphere of the planet, turn now your gaze and look directly into the Sun. The great light of the Sun is coming down and warming you. As this golden Sunlight comes in through your eyes, in through your head. Through your face, your senses, your crown chakra, down through all of your chakras in the spinal column.

And as the Solar energy is coming down through your body the Earth energy is also now moving up through the soles of your feet, balancing and grounding the great solar energy entering into your being. The Earth energy and Solar energy meets in all of your energy centers, meridians and chakras. You are the conduit between the earth and the sky. Healing, balancing, clearing and energizing you... Healing, balancing, clearing and energizing you, Healing, balancing, clearing and energizing you, continually.

And as you continue looking up you start to notice now that the rays of the Sun are calling you. As they come out radiating to meet you and they radiate within you as well. And as the light rays from the Sun radiate within you they start to draw you into the Sun as you are looking continually into it. Looking into the Sun and hovering towards it you come to meet the sun as you move into it.

There is a great clarity, a great light and a great warmth. A great love vibration that is here. The inside of the sphere of the Sun is lined with the Flower of Life geometry. A sacred geometry that speaks to all of creation. As you look around you notice that there are many masters here.

There are 12 Solar Angels who are very, very tall beings each one is holding a golden staff. Atop each staff is a Sacred Symbol that is moving with energy. These are the Sacred Solar Symbols. These are the symbols that helped give life to our solar system and life to our planet. As you look around you notice that there are tables filled with golden scrolls, golden tapestries and golden books.

Looking now in every direction in the greatest longest hall you have ever seen there are golden scrolls before you. Laid out here with symbols of gold vibrating with such harmony, warmth and light. There is a great central scroll that is unwinding and moving out before you like a slow moving path or stream. Ever continuously moving forth with symbols of gold woven into it. Unwinding out from the central table as it moves continually out and then gradually and steadily out of the sun.

Giving the energy and the golden symbols life as they move out by way of the Sun light to everything and everyone in the world, Solar system and star region of the Universe. Shining the sacred symbols that nourish creation.

As you continue to look around you see now that there are 4 masters coming from the distance to talk with you. There are 3 older men and one younger man in the middle.

The man on the left is Isaiah with a long white hair and beard. A very beautiful and loving man shining with his own light wearing a white robe trimmed in gold. On the right another master, a tall man with white hair and a beard wearing white known on Earth as Ezekiel. Both of these men were known as ancient masters of prophecy and visions.

Standing behind the 3 is Enoch an earth man who ascended into the Sun in ancient times. He is one of the Solar Angels and has a very strong and radiant presence shining with the spiritual fire light of Creator. Also wearing a flowing robe trimmed in the fire light of creation. Vibrating with light, power and wisdom.

A younger man who is with them in the center with long dark hair and a beard. His name is Isa. And he shines out with a beautiful bright light from his heart. The light that is pure love of Creator coming from the Great Central Sun.

Master Isa we ask you here and now for your Divine Healing, Love and Transmission of Light today. As we now take a few minutes to receive this Love Light Healing Transmission...*pause for a moment*

Isa we thank You for your healing Love it is so

obvious as the Love shines out from you that all things are made from Love in the Universe on all levels and in all dimensions.

As Isaiah on his left is also bringing now a Transmission of Light and Love through as Wisdom. Isaiah is bringing forth a vision of light and holding it in the air in front of you to look at. Take a few moments to look at this vision from the past...*pause for a moment*...Now Ezekiel on the right also radiating with a brilliant and soft light now brings forth a vision of the future as it is opened and hovers before you. Take a few moments to look at this vision from the future and watch it as it plays for you...*pause for a moment*...

Isa now brings forth a great portal of Light and Love that opens engulfing all 5 of you in the Eternal Now Moment. As the Eternal Now is radiating you are perceiving and experiencing that the vision on the left which is 'past' and the vision on the right which is 'future' are one in the same with the mind of God and the Universe. All moments, energy, visions, versions and dimensions are of the Divine. So you are able to perceive them through grace and peace within the moment.

At this time now Solar angelic master Enoch is standing behind and over the 3 masters displays now the emanations of Light as Love, Wisdom and Power from the Divine Solar Fire Light of Creation. And as all 4 of them are communicating energetically with you with Love and the Powerful Light of Eternity shining from their faces and their eyes, their minds, their lips and their hearts. Wisdom, Love and power of the Light. They are telling you stories in your heart and mind with energetic transmissions to help you through your journey in life. Relax now and receive these emanations of Wisdom, Light and Love through transmissions of Joy.

There are now 4 arc angels coming to greet you. As they come through the other side of the Sun. Arc Angel Metatron king of the angels, Arc Angel Michael the protector, Arc Angel Raphael the angel of healing, and Arc Angel Gabriel bringer of the Light. Each one of them with their aspects are adding to you, strengthening and integrating you with their energetic gifts and foundations....*pause for a few moments to receive these gifts...*

Now the 4 arc angels and the 4 Masters are all floating around you. All 8 are now all lifting you up very high within the middle of the Sun as you levitate up and are elevated there in the center of the Sun. They are now helping to translate the higher vibrations of this place in every way. And as you look now at the great solar angelic deities, these very, very tall beings with their staffs. These 12 angels are all forming now a great ring lining the inside of the sun. And their Light from the golden staffs and symbol that each one holds and represents starts to create a great focus of energy that comes to you.

You can feel the different vibrations of each symbol. Towards your body and your Soul and in all aspects of your being. As the energy now of each symbol flashes intermittently together. With Source Light Code Activation Frequencies. Source Light Code Activation Frequencies are coming in and lighting you up. Activating You and your Light Body.

As your Light Body is Activated you realize here in the Sun standing in front of the Solar Records, the Akashic Records of the Sun as Solaris and the Solaris system you realize that you know all things, that you are in touch with all things, that you are connected with all things because you are One with all things as the Solar angels continue to activate your light body in every way.

As the symbols come out to you and they change and morph, moving and dancing around and through your fields in patterns. Appearing, flashing and streaming as there is a symbol that is given for each one of your chakras. A Sacred Soul Symbol. A Sacred Akashic Symbol from within the Sun being anchoring your Soul, Light Body and the Solar energy into each chakra. This is a great achievement and blessing to receive these vibratory transmissions. As the solar deities at the outer ring of the perimeters of the sun flash their staffs 7 more times together activating you. This makes a total of 8 transmissions. Giving to you and releasing you at the same time.

Now as the activations are complete at this time, as the Arc Angels now move up into the light into the side of the Sun that points towards the center of creation. The Solar Angels open a window into space as the Arc Angels move out towards the edge of the Sun through this window towards the energy of the Great Central Sun.

The Souls from the Great Central Sun as parts of God, the Celestial Souls are coming in now. We see them like shooting stars, and as you witness you see them now everywhere present coming into the sun through this great window and coming straight through the sun out the other side towards Earth going to meet, enjoin with and harmonize with humanity.

Great Orbs of Light flooding in traveling from across outer space as they travel from the center of Creation. Moving into the Sun, through the Sun, leaving the Sun, utilizing the Sun as a great Divine Cosmic Star Gate. And as the Arc Angels stand on the edge of Creation as great ambassadors and you watch the Souls passing through the Sun you witness the great Blessings of Light here.

You now watch the Arc Angels move out as they move in the direction of the Great Central Sun as they are working with the Souls. As masters Isaiah, Isa, Ezekiel and Enoch give you their final messages, transmissions and blessings. And you feel yourself full of the solar energy and Light Activation from the Akashic Records within the Sun.

Knowing that these Universal symbols are coded with light technology frequency to give you the knowledge, wisdom and knowing and the inner knowing to project out, to radiate out great intuitive abilities whenever needed. Great Healing abilities whenever needed. So as the energy is radiating around you now and through you, now you start to float and levitate moving back out of the Sun.

Moving closer to the edge of the Sun as you're looking at everyone and everything there, all of the great beings. Now as you come out of the Sun, you feel like you're one step closer to knowing some of the ways in which the Universal energy flows and works. As you come out of the Sun and turning now you start your descent back towards the Earth. As the Earth is coming closer you come on back down to your Earth home. You feel Mother Earth's vibration coming closer to you now.

Coming back down to your continent, back to your country, back to your region and back down into your house and into your body. We thank the Divine Solar Deities, the Solar Angels, the Masters of Light, the Arc Angels and the Keepers of the Solar Akashic Records within the Sun for the access to these great intuitive emanations of Source Light Code Activation Frequencies. We Thank you in every way,

Om, Peace, Amen.

Exercise 6

JOURNEY
TO MEET THE
KEEPERS
OF THE
PLEIADIAN
RECORDS

*A*s we now prepare to Journey to the Akashic Records of the Pleiades, take a few moments to get yourself comfortable in the very best way possible. Sitting in a reclined position or laying down will be the best positions for you. A light blanket to cover the body to make it feel supported and safe is always helpful. Taking in now some long slow deep breaths and allowing every part of your body to relax.

Continually relaxing deeper and deeper moment by moment, feeling perfect relaxation filling your body.

As you continue your relaxation protocols. Relaxing and breathing relaxation into your feet, your legs, your midsection, breathing relaxation through your torso and your back, your hands and your arms, your shoulders up through your neck and your head. Relaxing all of your senses, your brain and relaxing now even your energy fields. Now that you have completed your relaxation procedure and protocol for your journey.

As you relax, down, down, down and you open. Opening and relaxing knowing that you are in protected space, sacred space, because you, my friend are doing this work from integrity and virtue. To know the Self and to gather Self knowledge.

There is now a great blue ball of energy in front of you. Focusing on this bright blue ball of light it starts to expand out. The blue light is now joined by a bright, bright white. So brilliantly shining out in all directions lighting up the whole room you are in with no shadows. As you continue to allow this Light, Your Light, to expand out past the walls and through the walls surrounding your home, the air space and deep down into the Earth.

Encompassing now the whole neighborhood and the town or region in which you live. Your blue and white Light orb continues out to engulf the state and then the whole country and finally the whole continent on which you live. As it expands now out across the ocean and out across North America and South America, Scandinavia and Europe, the United Kingdom all of these places are shining very brightly with your Light. As the energy continues to expand now and increase your energy engulfs all of Africa and all of the Middle East, continuing to expand out now. Engulfing Russia and the Far East. Engulfing China and Japan.

As your Light is so bright it is now engulfing Australia. Until the Eastern & Western hemispheres are shining very brightly in your Light.

Your Light has completely now engulfed the whole world. The whole planet earth is shining very brightly in your Light. And as the world is shining very brightly in your Light you may have noticed that you have ascended up over the planet. As as you are now here looking down at the planet from here in the space of the upper atmosphere.

As the world is turning and you're quietly looking at the Earth here from space. As the world is shining very bright in your blue and white Light you notice now that there are some bright orange points of light which are in different areas of the globe, some are farther apart, some are closer together. Take a moment to observe and study these points of orange light on the surface of the planet...These are all of your lifetimes on Planet Earth.

Turn now your vision and look directly up into the Sun. You notice now that there is bright golden energy coming out of the sun in spiral patterns. And as these spirals of Light come straight to You they come down through your body running in a spiral pattern. Cleansing you, healing you as it moves through you and spirals down towards the Earth. There is a conduit that reaches you from deep within the Earth as the great spiraling white Light is coming out of the Sun and coming down through you Healing You, Cleansing You and Clearing You. Notice as the energy coming out of the Sun continues that there is a great white shape or structure coming out of the Sun.

You realize that it is a very large ship made of Light. It bears the markings of the Galactic Federation. This ship is from the Pleiades and they have come to meet you here. With great respect and honor in observance of your Soul and your learning in life and the Universe as yourself and as part of God.

They have come to take you on a journey to one of your homes. As you start to float up towards the ship a great blue beam of light comes out of the ship. A pillar of light encompassing your body and gently lifts you up into this higher dimensional light ship. The energy is so high it feels so good and very light.

There is a very soft and comfortable high vibration that wants you to feel supported and comfortable like this all of the time. So as you continue through this ship and you arrive at the main center in the ship you realize that you're among friends, among brothers and sisters of the Galactic Federation of Light. Commander Ashtar of Ashtar Command is here, wearing a dark blue suit with bright blonde hair and firey blue eyes as he welcomes you aboard. Another very tall man with long blonde hair and blue eyes who looks very similar to Arc Angel Michael.

As you continue meeting and greeting everyone there are so many beings of Light here. Many Pleiadians are aboard among this crew. And there are many familiar faces. Your Pleiadian guides are here. There are Arc Angels. Christ Jesus, Isa, Jeshua is here. Many of the other Ascended Masters are here. Ancient masters from biblical times and Ancient masters from the Far East.

They are all communicating with you mentally and energetically through the Light. The Pleiadean guides that are here with you are so amazing and so much like you. Very human in appearance, very loving, very clear, compassionate and understanding as they say to you now we have come to take you to a very spacial place. We have come to take you home to visit the Pleiadean Hall of the Akashic Records of their star system. And as you're all standing before a great picture window in space. Here aboard this Light ship between the Earth and the Sun.

So now the leaders in this group of Pleiadians

send clear light intentions with their mind. They start to materialize the ship into even more light as it starts to vibrate with a very high frequency. They now turn the ship around and start the journey back through the star gate of the Sun. The ship and everyone on it including you is now moving through a portal, a wormhole in space. After a few minutes the ship comes to a great star system of the Pleiades. As the ship comes out of high speed and comes to a slow you are now approaching seven great planets of the Pleiades which are all in their own pattern here in space. Each planet is inhabited by a different group or faction of Pleiadians.

There is space travel back and forth between planets. And as you look now there is a great star like planet that is in the center of these planets. And this is where the light ship moves itself towards. As the ship moves closer to this station, your Pleiadians guides which are closest to you look at you and touching your shoulder and their 3rd eyes start to glow.

You and they together are beamed off of the ship and into this great central station between the Pleiadian planets. As you're here on this central station the energy is so high, it's also very compatable with you and very beneficial. It feels like home in so many ways. This place holds the energy of any and all lifetimes that you have ever lived within this star system as well as information about coming to and leaving the Pleiades. Of inhabitants and the Souls that incarnate on earth, many are Pleiadean. There are Pleiadeans on planet Earth in great numbers. Being welcomed aboard this central station that is circular. There is a great central hub which is like a great library and research area. There are books and scrolls and tablets here as well as computers and interfaces.

There are many antique versions of storing knowledge and information as well as huge collections of books scrolls and tablets and computers with holographic screens. You become very inspired as you are being welcomed by your guides that all of this is here for you to study. As you see the stars glowing in the background through the windows and you look around this central hub, it is floating and there are passageways that connect out to a great ring around this station.

This great ring houses the Pleiadian Elders. There are 13 Great Souls wearing very long robes and very tall beings. These are the ancient Pleiadians they are very, very old wisdom keepers. They command and attract great respect through the star systems as they have remained stationary here as watchers for a very long time, holding the vibrational core presence of the Pleiadians wisdom that radiates out to all of the 7 planets. They have been here watching over the Pleiadian Akashic Hall of Records and watching all of the Souls that come, all the Soul that move on and all Souls that stay and advance themselves through this civilization.

As your guides are with you, one of the Ancient wisdom keepers comes from the outer ring hovering and floating now into the central library. As they walk you through the library you are now given access to the Pleiadian Records and especially your own Records here. As you are brought to a Great Book of incarnations that has a coinciding holographic computer screen. You look at your lists of families as you are shown your lifetimes here in the Pleiadian star system. You are also shown your names here. As you are now very aware that you have been here. Take a few moments to view the holographic screen and to look into and to remember from within this place your history here...

The Wisdom Keeper starts talking to you about the differences and the similarities between the Pleiades and Earth and your Soul and what you learned and embodied from this place. What you have experienced.

Take a few moments for this conversation to take place between you and the Pleiadian Wisdom Keepers and for the information to come in...

You may ask the question here "What is the nature of my lifetimes and destiny among the stars?

You are receiving great knowledge at this time and great downloads of wisdom and ancient knowledge into your Soul. Take a few moments to let all of this information come in for you....

There is a Pleiadian alphabet of Soul Symbols that are being generated from the center of the this great corridor in this circular chamber. These holographic symbols are Pleiadian Akashic Soul Symbols. They are very unique in their own style. As they are showing these lights symbols they are also giving you information about your Life Path among the stars as a Soul and also about your assignment on Planet Earth.

They are bringing downloads of information to you from the Pleiadian Records that benefits your current and future journey on all levels. They are giving you great insight about the nature of your journey in every way. And as you are becoming filled up with the energy here and the activations among the stars.

The energy of the Pleiadian Akashic Records that you are accessing is also being charged and amplified by the cosmic starlight of the surrounding space and stars which you can also feel.

As they have filled you up with energy and the messages and stories of deep knowing and remembrances of your times among the stars and your previous visits to this place.

The Great Pleiadian Wisdom Keepers have

special messages for you that they are transmitting to you by light code frequency. You see it as a flash or burst of light coming from each one. They are giving you a blessing. You have received great activations from the ancient Pleiadian tribes as well as from your Akashic Soul Records and Star Records here within the library. You will become aware of this information as it is needed throughout your Akashic practices and throughout your life's journey.

As the Wisdom Keepers bid you adieu they now move back to there respective stations of the circular hub in the outer ring.

The Pleiadian guides that are with you are telling you that it is time to go back to the light ship now. The vibration here is so interesting, inviting and comfortable you almost want to stay longer. Though you know you will be back and that you can use this guided process to come back. So agreeing with them you turn and start to make your way back with the guides as you are floating to the outer ring of the station. Where then you are beamed back aboard of the Light Ship.

As you are back on board now with all of the brothers and sisters of the Galactic Federation of Light and all of the familiar faces and great beings. As this Light ship running on their mind power is turned around now and starts to increase in velocity it moves into hyper speed and makes it's way through a hyper space window as it approaches light speed many times over. Moving through a wormhole in space and after several minutes the ship of Light emerges through our Sun. The Pleiadian members and the Galactic Federation members are so thankful and joyful that they have gotten to connect with you and participate in your Great Journey. They are forever in gratitude and forever in service of You and your Life and Soul's journey.

They now escort you from the ship through a great beam of blue Light all the way back down to planet Earth. All the way back down to your home and with great healing energy, spiritual activation and cosmic energy. They beam you back down directly into your home and into your body.

So it is with great knowledge, great reverence and recognition as you now feel the Light ship has returned to their regularly scheduled duties and returned back through the Sun.

We thank the Galactic Federation of Light and we thank all of the Pleiadians and all of the great beings who are always here to help and assist us in every way and everyday.

Om, Peace, Namaste, Amen.

Exercise 7

MEETING
WITH THE
COUNCIL
OF
LIGHT

*A*s we now prepare to for a meeting with the Council of Light, take a few moments to get yourself comfortable in the very best way possible for you. Sitting in a reclined position or laying down will be the best positions for you. A light blanket to cover the body to make it feel supported and safe is always helpful. Taking in now some long slow deep breaths and allowing every part of your body to relax.

Continually relaxing deeper and deeper moment by moment, feeling perfect relaxation filling your body.

As you continue your relaxation protocols. Relaxing and breathing relaxation into your feet, your legs, your midsection, breathing relaxation through your torso and your back, your hands and your arms, your shoulders up through your neck and your head. Relaxing all of your senses, your brain and relaxing now even your energy fields. Now that you have completed your relaxation procedure and protocol for your journey. As you relax, down, down, down and you open. Opening and relaxing knowing that you are in protected space, sacred space, because you, my friend, are doing this work from integrity and virtue. To know the Self and to gather Self knowledge.

There is now a great white sphere of Light energy in front of you. Focusing on this bright white sphere of Light it starts to expand out. So brilliantly shining out in all directions lighting up the whole room you are in with no shadows. As you continue to allow this Light, Your Light, to expand out past the walls and through the walls surrounding your home, the air space and deep down into the earth.

Encompassing now the whole neighborhood and the town or region in which you live. Your white Light orb continues out to engulf the state and then the whole country and finally the whole continent on which you live. As it expands now out across the ocean and out across North America and South America, Scandinavia and Europe, the United Kingdom all of these places are shining very brightly with your Light. As the energy continues to expand now and increase your energy engulfs all of Africa and all of the Middle East, continuing to expand out now. Engulfing Russia and the Far East. Engulfing China and Japan. As your light is so bright engulfing now Australia. Until the Eastern and Western hemispheres are shining very brightly in your Light.

Your Light has completely now engulfed the whole world. The whole planet Earth is shining very brightly in your Light. And as the world is shining very brightly in your Light you may have noticed that you have ascended up over the planet. As as you are now here looking down at the planet from here in the space of the upper atmosphere.

As the world is turning and you're quietly looking at the earth here from space. As the world is shining very bright in your bright white light you notice now that there are some bright green points of light which are in different areas of the globe, some are farther apart, some are closer together. Take a moment to look at and study these points of green light on the surface of the planet...These are all of your lifetimes on Planet Earth.

Turn now your vision and look directly up into the Sun. You notice now that there is bright golden energy coming out of the Sun in spiral patterns. And as these spirals of Light come straight to You they come down through your body running in a spiral pattern.

Cleansing you, healing you as it moves throughout you and spirals down towards the Earth. There is a conduit that reaches you from deep within the Earth as the great spiraling white light is coming out of the Sun and coming down through you Cleansing You, Clearing You and Healing You.

As you are looking into the Sun there is a great glowing warmth that's coming from the Sun. The white and golden light of the Sun is calling you through your senses. It is calling you to come forward.

As you continue looking into the Sun you feel yourself starting to levitate directly towards the Sun. As you move closer the energy is helping to bring you even closer to it. The Sun is so large and you can really sense the grand presence of this solar giant as you move closer now. Being pulled directly into the Sun you start to feel the sense of a longing for home. As you start to hear a voice now silently in your mind, a very large yet soft voice it says "I'm calling you home for a little while."

As you start to come into the middle of the Sun this time it is different, you see it purely as a place of light. It is very rejuvenating to be inside this great solar conduit of cosmic energy. As you look up and around you in every direction you see connecting portals of light that are shining out from the Sun like the rays. These are actual cosmic pathways that connect all of the stars and planets together in a great directory.

Through this perspective view of the Great Directory of the stars and planets all interconnected with each other you see can feel a great sense of Oneness like you have just touched into another level of understanding through the perception and observation of this great star directory.

As a Soul of Light you are now being called home back to your Source of existence. As the Great Light fills you now and your Soul field is glowing around you as it becomes your vehicle of Light. It becomes very easy to maneuver within your Soul Body as it is being recognized and acknowledged by the Universe as a living part of the whole.

As you move up and directly through the center of the Sun you are being called through the largest connecting portal of Light. As light beings gather around now inside the Sun they are signaling you that you are fine and will be perfectly safe on this journey that you are about to take. You are now pulled through the portal as you are flying very gently and gliding faster and faster to what feels like a great sense of home or a great sense of peace.

Moving faster and faster you are aware of the cosmos as you're moving through the white Light portal traveling very safely up, up and away. After a few moments you reach a great opening in front of the largest Sun you could possibly fathom. The Great Central Sun. The Essence of All Originating

Souls of Creation. You have arrived at the center of the Universe and the center of Creation.

There is a Great Light, a very soft light here. As you move out in front of the originating Light of Creation. You can feel the living love light essence of the Great Central Sun. It is living and breathing with the pure essence of creation. Divine living loving energy of God Source of which you are part. Your Soul came from this place. And as you're visiting here you can feel the deep soft healing energy of this place filling you up.

As you look into the surface glow of the Central Sun you see and feel the great soft pink, white and gold energy emanating from this place. It feels so good to be back home to this origin from whence you came on your journey across the stars. As you look more closely you now see that Great Central Sun is comprised completely of Souls. It is made of living beings and as they move and shine together in unison you see them coming up out of the surface and then back down into the collective.

At this time there is a great beam that shines from the top of the Sun through and out the bottom of the Sun as a great pole or portal of Light. As it shines in a direct vertical beam across the Universe it now opens up into two cones of energy. These cones continue to widen, open and flatten until they come down and meet each other in the middle in what make the most brilliant flash of light that you have ever witnessed. As there is a great flash of Light and it fades there are now hovering before you in front of the Great Central Sun 12 great beings. These are the Council of Light members. They are illumined from within themselves as these great beings of power, wisdom and light as Giants of Light are all here as you have traveled all this way to witness their presence and to come before them. As they start to speak to you in your heart and in your mind they have great messages for your life.

"It is you that have traveled so far on your journey to meet with us. That in and of itself shows great courage, strength and perseverance. Your origin is of the pure light and we have brought you here to remember that. In your lives and among the stars and your Earth lives, you have become confused through the projections of 3 dimensional reality. You have become involved emotionally and sometimes karmically to great lengths."

"We have brought you here to recognize you for all of your incarnational work. As you feel now this great light energy and think back to the Earth, what would feel like this energy on the earth plane? Yes the ocean, would give to your senses and your body energetically in the same way that we are lifting you up here and now. With Divine vibrations of Love. It is important for you to receive from the Earth what she has to offer you while you are still there."

"All of your limiting thought projections that you have created or involved yourself in...All of your emotional patterns that seem to have you in a holding pattern...All of your life issues that you have cocreated as lessons and limitations are to be systematically surpassed when you are ready. These are illusionary to you as the Great Emanating Soul that you are."

"You are easily able to move past these Self induced parameters. As you are witnessing yourself now in our presence as pure light, you now know your true Essence once again and you will carry this essence back with you to your Earth life and your Earth home. This vibrational experience will remind you that you can still feel this part of your grand being even though you will be back on the earth plane. We are here to acknowledge your Light and to light you up, not to judge you from the worldly situations that you have found yourself in. As you now understand we have no judgement for you. You can truly release all burdens and carry this Great Light home with you."

"You are the Light and you are Divine. Take this time to receive the True Emanations of the Light..."

"We want to give you a gift of activation. We will activate your Light Body and activate your Merkabah or vehicle of Light."

So as you hover before this Great Council of 12, they start to shines beams of light from their eyes.

In rhythmic patterns which cause your DNA in all of the cells of your light body to awaken. As your energy now glows and sings like the Light Beings hovering before you.

There is also now a great rainbow field of colors as they are now creating a 3 pointed tetrahedron pyramid of light over your head that comes down around your body. As an inverted 3 pointed tetrahedron pyramid under your body that comes up around your body to interlock with the other pyramid. These two interwoven pyramids are spinning. The top pyramid is spinning clockwise representing male/positive charged energy. The bottom pyramid is spinning clockwise representing female/negative charged energy.

As they are turning in opposite directions around your body they create a great rainbow light field representing a six pointed tetrahedron star. This is your light vehicle or **Merkabah** which has been activated for you by them as a gift to You for making the great journey.

"You may return to your world now Great Soul" they say collectively to you. "We have given you this gift of a Light vehicle because through our love we knew it would carry you safely home. It will also be a great gift of travel that you can use to go other places in your Akashic meditations or dream journeys. It will also bring you back here to replenish your energy when you need to make it back home for a revitalizing visit. We will be here for you. We will always be here."

"Now go and take back with you all that you have learned from us on a vibrational, emotional, mental, cellular and energetic level. Be the Light that you came out from this Source to be. The energy here will follow you back through your Sun and will always subtly whisper to you through your Sun. So Be Alive and Love with all you have, Enjoy and be creative. We bid you farewell for now and look forward to your return." As the Light Council of 12 now moves back into the Great Central Sun and takes their place in the Essence of the Light of Creation.

With great passion and with great love and inspiration, you start your journey home as looking at the Great Sun to remember this pure love place in the Universe. So turning now in your great spinning star field of light, your Merkabah you start your journey back the portal of light in the Star Directory that connects you to your home world Sun. Moving along the portal with grace and ease you feel as though you have really accomplished something. You have revisited and regained a great piece of yourself. Re-energized and even re-invented your Soul's journey with the help of the Great Council.

Moving at the speed of light you feel like you're being softly carried along on the wings of the Light. As you return to our local Sun you can feel the energy inside the local Sun and you know it's vibration well. As you continue on out of the Sun moving past Mercury and Venus you now see the big blue marble known as home. As you start to come closer to the Earth you really get to appreciate the beauty of the Earth from here in space.

As you continue down in your vehicle of rainbow light, you come down in to the atmosphere and pass over the great oceans and continents. Coming to your homeland you now feel the great warmth of coming home as you come down to your local area and down to your home as you come back down in through the ceiling and back into your physical body when you reintegrate your total being.

You can feel your body and energy fields vibrating with the Great Light and the changes that have taken place. You know that you will not soon forget this great journey home to meet the Council of 12, the council of your brothers and sisters of light. Relax and enjoy your new energy activations and upgrades. Om, Peace, Namaste, Amen.

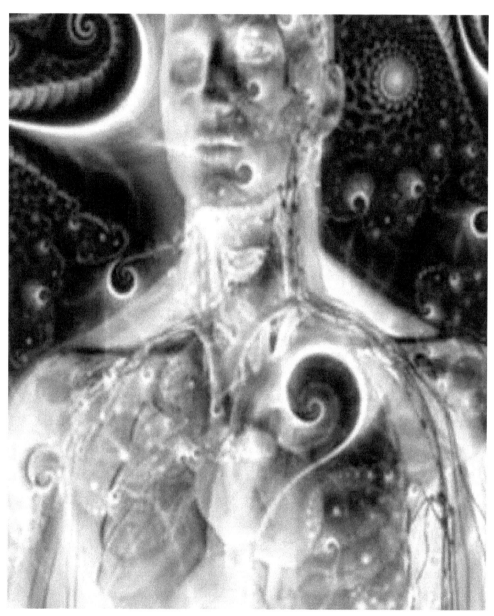

AS YOU BECOME AWARE OF NEW HIDDEN LEVELS OF YOUR SOUL ENERGY INVOLVED IN OTHER DIMENSIONAL REALITIES, YOU ARE LEARNING OF THE NEW AND TRUE DYNAMICS OF THE WAY THAT SOUL ENERGY ACTUALLY WORKS.

Chapter 12

MultiDimensional Healing & Travel within the Records

*T*here is a place within each of us that is part of a great joy. A consciousness of Universal Love that permeates every living fiber of our being. As we come into the world we are pure innocence. We are in complete nurtured support and harmony inside the womb of our mother until the first levels of separation in our new life start to occur. As we start to experience the external world and our surroundings we have to learn to become adapted to this new world.

From the original innocence of the womb out and into a new and strangely different outer world. We operate from the innocence of each moment in this brave new world and so we adapt and learn to take in all that we can. All that comes into contact with us leaves an impression and as we grow we start to leave impressions on our surroundings as well, though the exchange is not equal as a smaller being.

Our external world tends to have the upper hand in influencing our responses to it. As we continue to grow we also bring with us preferences and experiences from other time lines or past lives. These preferences from past lives are often times accompanied by karmas or life lessons that we have brought with us through our Soul to work on as karmas and lessons through observation and participation. As we have new life experiences we start to have responses and reactions to the world around us. Our responses to our world create our lives and our character. Sometimes we even create new karmas in the course of trying to work out old issues or lessons from past lives.

The greatness of our Soul peering through our windows to the world the whole time. Waiting for the right timing and moments to set everything straight and into a more continual balance. As we have a mixture of the Soul's radiantly divine nature and the ego's crafty antics, we tend to spiral back and forth between the two until we either naturally learn our own lessons of balance or we start to learn directly about the dynamics of the Soul and ego that brings us more perfect alignment and radiant balance in each moment.

Self acceptance of all parts of the mind, body and spirit brings comfort, peace, and inspiration which allows us to radiate joy and love out into the world.

We are truly multi-dimensional beings. We have come from other lifetime incarnations up into the Akashic Records as a Soul to review those past lifetimes and then back down again into human form. As we learn to live, laugh, learn, cry, and to love all over again with the hopefulness of our own Higher Self and the Teachers on the other side of learning to do things uniquely different or learning to respond to similar situations or variations therein differently.

In this way we are making progress as a part of God on our way back to enlightenment or Divine Source. In so many ways we are connected to our multidimensional selves. Our Soul is directly connected to all of our 'other selves' through the Eternal Now moment. Continually streaming in the background of our 'here and now' lives in this reality.

As we are connected to these other more silent parts of our beings that we tend to isolate as 'past lives' the greater part of our selves, the Higher Self and the Soul along with the Higher Mind know differently. These parts of our integrated being now that we are more deeply connected to our other selves in other time lines. The challenge is that these other lifetime selves can sometimes have influences on the current Self through the Soul's connection to this body and reality.

When this occurs much of the time we are oblivious to it. Unless we are connected in and are working with our own Book of Life within the Akashic Records. If we have influences whether known or unknown, physical or energetic, then we are able to work with these influences and respond accordingly to our benefit. If we are not able to fathom what's going on with the influences of our existence, often times it can be that there is a silent program running in another life that is drawing energy from us in this reality.

When this happens, through my studies and sessions with others I have witnessed sometimes a true befuddlement within individuals as they have tried to figure out what's holding them back in life either physically, emotionally, abundantly or in relationships. Often these silent other realities are causing a draw or a pull that the Soul is naturally working at balancing. Though the Soul is aligned in the 'here and now' within this current time line and reality through your current body, mind and senses it is silently in touch with parts of us experiencing other realities and other lifetimes.

So we may ask is there a special need or important reason for this balancing act of another lifetime that's pulling on this body and reality or is it inconsequential? If the latter is the case then we can clear the pathway and release that reality to it's own existence. We are able to seal the doorway or window so to speak between the other reality, the Soul and this reality in a beneficial and healing way with love, good intentions and harm to no one.

As we separate or partition the lifetime realities more of the Soul's energy start to again flow through the present time individual's consciousness and body. And this is the quietly hidden approach that can help us move forward when we've tried everything else and nothing has seemed to work.

This Soul dynamic can have a silent pull or influence that is similar to an astrological influence. As you continue to stop, look and listen in your life at different subtle influences through deep levels of introspection we are led to finding this seemingly magical needle in a haystack.

As you become aware of these new hidden levels of your Soul energy balancing operations or involved in other dimensional realities, you are learning of the new and true dynamics of the way that Soul energy actually works. This new look into the workings of the Soul also brings other broader spectrum activities as well. Soul energy can also be operating in multiple physical bodies just as easily as one body and within the same area or different regions of the world. Think about that for a moment.

When we think about going into the other side or the dream world in comparison to the waking state as we are present here, in some ways this seems more normal as a way of working clairvoyantly.

As this may be a new concept for your mind to grasp it can also be expanding. Think of the possibilities that can be achieved by learning, experiencing and observing through more than one body and set of senses simultaneously. The potential is phenomenal and especially if these soul enjoined other self versions are somehow connected in the same family or working together in some ways.

As we move up into the Akashic Records and connect with our own Book of Life the important dynamic to know is that it's natural and organic for the process of your Soul field to be bolstered and it's radiant presence increased.

Working with the Akashic Records and your very own Book of Life within the Records is the only way that I know of that this dynamic of Soul Radiance Increase is available. These are silent and higher dynamics withing the Akashic Records that you achieve on a Soul level from working within them. When you are working on this level you will be tuning in and listening to the subtle increases in your Soul's field as well as an invitation from the Ascended masters and the higher beings of healing to start working on a more evolved level. This is a level of healing that you can't get in any other way.

As we travel up to the Records we open a portal of knowledge, wisdom and information that starts to become available to us and this continues to open us as we do the work. So as we go up into the Records the Soul field comes down around and into our physical body more. This is a unique expansion process. We can also bring the Records down to us here in the dimensional fields that surround us. If you are prone to leaving the body through old traumas or not wanting to be here in on physical plane this can be a unique way of grounding the energies. This will keep you present here locally with your body while you bring the Records of your Book of Life down through the Portal of Light in order to work with you here locally live and in person.

Also well noted that going up to the Akashic Records and your Book of Life therein will give you a target location. When we move about continuously leaving the body because of traumas this is a form of energetic escapism. By giving the mind and the Soul a target location we develop an etheric sense of home that we can literally count on and depend on because it's a very real place. And every time we practice to go there or project ourselves there the Akashic Records and our Book of Life will be there for us. In the essence of healing and learning these connections are nothing short of stellar for us.

EXERCISE: JOURNEY UP INTO THE RECORDS & BRING THE RECORDS DOWN AROUND YOU

As prepare yourself to meditate, get into a relaxed position with a glass of water close by and a blanket to cover the physical body to help it feel safe and relaxed is sometimes helpful. As you relax down into this exercise, relaxing by breathing healing energy into every part of the body, starting with the feet and ending with the head and face. As you continue to relax and breath, relaxing down even deeper, create a ball of white Light right over your body and from this great Light which is your light follow a thread of light straight up from this light. Follow it all the way up, straight away into the heavens.

As you follow it up through the sky and into the clouds the earth is falling away. As you continue on up through the clouds, you come to a place above the clouds which is the inside of a great temple, you have arrived at your target location of the Higher Dimensions, the Great Hall of the Akashic Records. Feel the energy there in the Great Hall. It feels like home, it feels like you and the true essence of your Soul energy. Just take some time to be in this energy and familiarize yourself with it. As you stay within the energy of the Akashic Records let the energy work with you in the subtle ways that your Soul knows best. After you are here for a little while, give gratitude for the experience knowing that you will be back soon.

As you follow the white thread all the way back down through the ethers into your body the home of your Soul, bring back with you the healing energy of the Akashic Records and your Book of Life and just let it settle into your whole being. Notice how it feels as you enjoy this new integration.

After a few moments of reintegration take yourself now back into a state ready to integrate with the Records in a new way. As you relax now and receive, see feel and experience a great portal of light opening from above. As this great light pillar comes down feel the brightness of it. As it increases in intensity everything else in the room becomes a bit dimmer as it moves back. Your main focus now becomes this great pillar of Light. See now a great book appear in front of you on a pedestal or a table. As you look at this book it emanates with a Divine Presence that is the same as you experienced as you travelled up into the Records.

This book is shining with healing energy and has messages to give directly to you as you tap into it. The great vibrations that are coming through the Book are the same as your Soul Vibrations. You are once again being added to in your Soul Essence and in very subtle higher dynamics. Enjoy this energy as you stay within it for a few moments. Ask some questions as you have brought your connection to your Book of Life down into your presence....*take a few moments to watch and listen.*

As the Book moves back into the light, the Great pillar of light fades back into the normal light of the room. You are returning now to your local reality and your waking state. Welcome Home.

Chapter 13

LEARNING
TO READ
THE AKASHIC
LANGUAGE

*I*n the higher dimensions there are a multitude of symbols and geometries that have been translated into physical reality. These symbols have been drawn and written in the spiritual cultures across the globe throughout time. They have been used to inspire and designate sacred practices of our Earth's civilizations participating with the Divine Universal Intelligence known as God.

We have sought, as incarnate beings, to find our origins as we forever ask the question "Who Am I? Those Souls who have been courageous enough to look for answers to these questions have often spent large parts of their lives studying, praying, meditating and writing about their experiences. Throughout the languages of the cultures of our world exist sacred characters and special words. In many cultures of our planet there are sacred geometries and mandalas that represent portals into Sacred Space where we connect with the Divine. This is where God, The Divine, Universal Cosmic Intelligence meet us in our reality. These geometries within space can create a field of sacred energy in which we may bask.

The monks of ancient times and today have sacred rites with geometries and mandalas. Some of these consist of visual meditations and also include sacred mantras. As these meditations and rites are accomplished there are many inner planes, worlds and places that the practitioners are able to tap into. Indeed one of these special places is none other than the Akashic Records.

The Akashic Records is comprised of a symbolic language of light. These symbols which hale from the higher dimensions of light and specifically from the Akashic Records libraries are comprised solely of and radiating pure light. These are the symbols which all of our written languages come from. When you look into the Records of the Light through visions or dreams you may see these symbols coming to you. The Akashic Soul symbols that radiate energy. These forms bring to us change, as the Light is literally living and moving with energy. It moves, changes, transforms and morphs into different segments of info. Sometimes we may see only one special symbol or several. We may even see multiple streams of characters and symbols. I usually refer to this as a download. When we see or experience streams of special symbols there is a reason for it. We are being communicated with from our Soul's Records or from the Keepers of the Records in ways that can give us subtle upgrades. It can help us move forward in life or to commence a new part of our life and our studies.

Take a moment and go back to a special character or symbol that you have seen in your mind. If you haven't seen one before create one now. Look at all the nuances of this symbol. What does it feel like energetically? Does it have a message for you? Is it a general message or is it specific to you?

As you look into the light now in your mind's eye are there other symbols that are following it or accompanying it? Are they moving and alive? Look closely and continuously into the light and let your minds eyes guide you. Allow your inner vision to open.

Create in your mind now and visualize a great portal of Light coming down from above. Just allow the goodness of the Light to connect with you. Know that all the information that you will be getting is coming from this Light. See now before you in the deep indigo blue space before you symbols forming out of the light.

You may see one central character or symbol

forming that is talking to you energetically. How does it feel? What is the message? Allow yourself to receive a message through thoughts, words or feelings. This is one of your Soul Symbols from the Akashic Library of Languages of Light. As you tap into this symbol notice that there are other symbols around it. They may appear as a stream or a line of characters or symbols. They may also look to be somewhat like a number or alphabetical letter. Similar to our known dialects but then again different than you have seen before. We could say that all written dialects come from these symbols, characters and language.

As you look now at these symbols you may see that they have similar qualities and subtle meanings as emanations of light that create thought and emotion. They are interactive with our thoughts and feelings. As we vibe into them more they subtly change and morph.

They are speaking to us through a conversation from the Light of the Akashic Language. This language has both subtle and more pronounced images within it that are conveying the Light. The symbols, images and characters subtly changes as new strokes are added or taken away. We may compare this to the interpretations of the Holy Bible. Is it literal or symbolic? That is usually the question or even argument that has went on for ages concerning the Bible's quotes and passages.

In much the same way when messages are given from the Records during a channelled reading, they can be either literal or figurative and sometimes translate as both. You will understand what I mean when you experience it first hand. When you receive a message that seems literal and so as you move forward in life you experience the message playing out in your life in a totally different way than you expected. Though the message that was given may translate both literally and figuratively.

As you study the Akashic language and work at interpreting it's many facets and meanings you will come to see the comparison between the Language of Light and the way that the many interpretations of the Holy Scriptures have had multiple perspectives.

As you start to practice these interpretive symbolic sections of energetic language, you will be finding your way into the process of the learning, experiencing and into the channelling process itself. This is key in your practice. As you look into the symbols and their groupings you will uncover your own style or creative dialect of energy messaging. This may be personal to you and your own psyche. Though as you compare your channelled symbols to those of others you will find that the styles will be different and some of the characters and symbols will be the same or very similar. These are the Soul symbols from the Central Akashic Library Hub.

In this you will come to know and understand that it is your own style and language that is important because it's as much about the act of your channelling of the energetic symbols and messages as it is about trying to figure out a foreign dialect that is alien to you.

Though this can happen in many ways. So far we have approached it solely from the creative mind of inquiring about the symbols as they are created on the screen of your mind. This is the interactive way of the mind field working with the frequencies coming in morphing them and flowing with them as in helping to create them in the mind's eye.

The other end of this spectrum is receiving direct downloads of symbols and automatically knowing what each and every one of them says. Receiving a direct message which you trust because it is like someone is speaking to you or writing you a letter. Also message interpretations can happen anywhere in between these two styles. So enjoy the process of creating as you look into the mysts and view the Symbols that speak through your Soul. As you start interpreting the symbols and receiving messages that influence your path you will become inspired to forge forward into continually new territories.

You want to allow the messages to come in as you look at the symbols. What you want to be careful with is that your ego is not making things up in accordance with the lower mind. Practice reading without conflict, tension, stress or fears. Just as in meditation we seek to move past these aspects of the mind to have a more peaceful and streaming experience.

There are many symbolic and pictographic ancient dialects which are closer to the symbols of the Akashic Light Language. Here are a few images of some of these languages.

EGYPTIAN HIEROGLYPHS

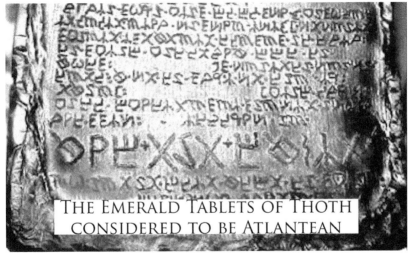

THE EMERALD TABLETS OF THOTH
CONSIDERED TO BE ATLANTEAN

ANCIENT CHINESE DIALECT
SIMILAR TO LEMURIAN

PRE-SUMERIAN DIALECT

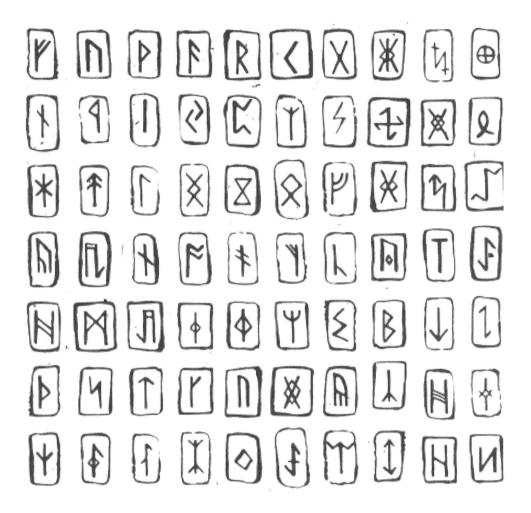

THE NORDIC RUNES

Many of these symbols and characters are very similar from ancient culture to culture. Take a few moments to look over these symbols before you go into the following meditation to find your own special symbols coming to you from your Soul within the Akashic Records.

Exercise 8

Channelling the Symbols of the Akashic Records

This is a guided meditation process. Please read through the script and then get comfortable and practice the inner guided exercise of accessing the Soul's Akashic symbols for your practice and your personal self development.

As you get comfortable please remain stationary in a relaxed position. You can either recline in a comfortable chair or couch. Or you can lay down with a good pillow for support of your neck and back. As you relax start to breathe in and out very comfortably with long slow deep peaceful breaths. Relaxing down, down, down. As you continue to relax you are telling your body, mind and spirit to all come together in a peaceful harmony. You find yourself drifting closer to the veil of sleep as you gather your senses somewhere between wake and sleep. Now as you find yourself balancing in this space, find yourself now in a beautiful outdoor setting. You are on the beach. It is the perfect day and temperature. You are in a very relaxed state. This is your day, place and time. Not a care in the world.

As you pan your vision to the right slowly and then look to the left slowly you see the beach spreading out for miles as it disappears into the distance. See now the ocean in front of you with the waves gently splashing into the beach as the great ocean disappears into the horizon line. It's like looking into forever.

As you look out across the great body of water it is very relaxing to you and very expanding. You see the blue of the sky over head that comes down to meet the horizon line. There are white puffy clouds against the backdrop of a bright blue sky slowly moving past.

As you now look into the horizon the sun is setting with a beautifully soft and golden light. As it quietly hangs over the ocean focus your mind's eye on the energy coming from the sun. There are what appears to be symbols coming from the sun. As a great symbol of light comes out of the sun It hovers before you as if to greet you. It is bringing you a message of energy. Take a few moments now to look at the energy of the symbol and it's form.

This is your Soul Symbol. What is the energy of

your Soul Symbol telling you? As you receive an energy transmission from this symbol of light it comes closer as it is absorbed into your Soul field and dissipates from your vision.

There are now new symbols coming out of the sun. As the symbols come out of the sun they set on the horizon just below the Sun. They are bring you a message. What is the message of the symbols for you here today at this time.

As the energy of the ocean surges with the energy of Solaris the Sun, a wonderful field of energy is created as you are reading the symbols. Notice what they look like. What are the shapes? What does the energy of the string or group of symbols have to share with you? Allow the messages to come in. After you have connected with the symbols you can also ask for the energy of the symbols to simplify themselves into a language of your choice. As words form you can read them. The guides may also bring audible messages for you. You may also experience a direct knowing from the symbols or messages. These are personal messages just for you. So take your time and relax and absorb the messages and energy that they have to offer.

As you receive messages some of them may be long range life time messages or they may pertain to a special segment of your life. The symbols can bring messages of coming events or they can bring inspiring messages and thoughts to help you in creating your path and moving forward. Continue to practice receiving these messages from the Light Language of the Akashic Records and see how it lights up your life path. You are sure to be supported in yet another deep and interesting way from within your Book of Life and the Akashic Records.

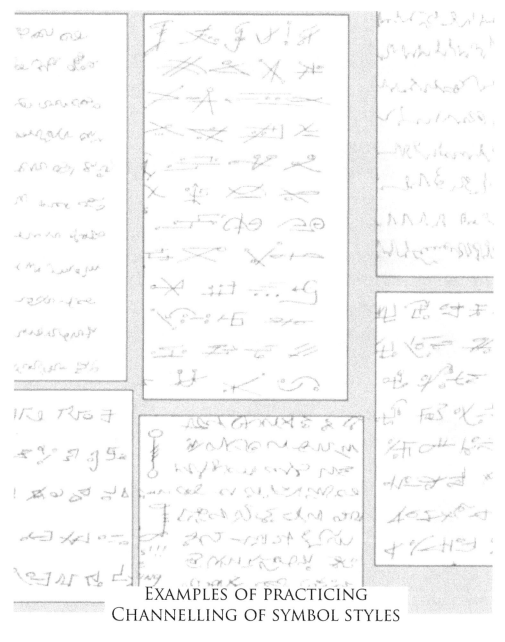

EXAMPLES OF PRACTICING
CHANNELLING OF SYMBOL STYLES

243

THE GOD SOUL ENERGY WHICH IS YOU, AND COMES THROUGH YOUR SENSES IN THE HERE AND NOW INSPIRES THE GREAT KNOWING OF THE SELF THAT IS REFERRED TO IN ALL OF THE ANCIENT TEXTS.

Chapter 14

SOUL GROUPS SOUL MATES & TWIN FLAMES WITHIN THE RECORDS

*W*ithin the Universe is a huge continual tapestry of Souls which are constantly and continually interwoven. As we look at the immensity of all Souls in human form here on the planet now and Souls that have previously incarnated. What do you think these numbers are? At the time of this book written we are looking at now 7.8 billion people incarnate in human form. The magnitude of so, so many Souls coming in and out of lifetime cycles here in the 3rd dimensional reality on planet Earth alone is staggering. Think of that now across the whole Universe!

The dynamic of Souls constantly incarnating en mass brings with it other continual situations. There is the need for karmic connections between Souls. The cause and effect of the Universe is the cosmic template for all of these Souls in their call and response to situational interactions with each other.

Not just one pair or a few pairs of Souls with karmic destinies but try on 7.8 billion Souls plus. So if it were just one soul that each person had karma with in one of their lifetimes, that would make roughly 3.9 billion pairs of Souls having a karmic cause and effect interaction for the greater learning of the collective Soul experience in the Greater Mind of God. The interactions between Souls and groups of Souls is beyond being counted because it is ever changing with creation in situational responses.

Most Souls have multiple interactions with more than one Soul on a karmic level whether negative or positive. The Universe, God and all of the Guides involved with all of these Souls including the Arc Angels and the Ascended Masters have a hand in helping to align with these meetings. So you can imagine if it isn't quite convenient to us in the moment for a karmic interval to take place, think about the immensity of trying to align all of the passing Souls with each other. Referring to Souls incarnate and Souls in between lives.

The scheduling process that takes place and the massive communications constantly between all parties involved to make this happen is in concept nothing short of astonishing. This is why the idea and template of the Tapestry of Humankind is represented within the Akashic Records.

As grand as this seems there are several more perspectives to the story. The next synchronistic aligning dynamic to perceive is that All Souls travel in groups of 12. On the other side there is an energy matrix connection for all 12 Souls in your personal Soul group. Meanwhile some of these Souls may be incarnate and some currently out of body.

The next dynamic happening simultaneously is that there are 12 Soul groups of 12 together. Each 12 Soul Groups has an over Soul. And each 12 sets of Over Souls has what is referred to in the ancient texts as the Monad which could also be called the Over Over Soul. On the other side of the veil you are starting to get the big picture of the carousels of carousels cascading in great numbers together. While some remain there and some remain here on this side of the veil. Constantly changing places and interweaving together.

So now we will add another dynamic that is also taking place simultaneously. The matrix of the bloodline of your current ancestry and the family tree. You are connected to your current bloodline all the way back to the ancient ancestors through your DNA coming from your mother and father. Each of them has their mothers and fathers and so the tree goes all the way back through history. Often times a Soul who has been experiencing the same bloodline will also try to reincarnate again as another family member in the same bloodline if possible.

Your current incarnation is tethered, if you will, through your DNA and also something called the 'Body Spirit' Your body spirit is the original base part of your Soul which has undergone jumping from lifetime to lifetime, in body and out of body carrying with it the remembrance of all of the body tissue cellular memories as well as family and karmic memories.

The Celestial Soul is the cosmic part of your Soul which has come from God as a finger print of God or the Divine. This part of your Soul has all of the memories of all of the other star systems that you've lived in. This is the higher part of your Soul that also has a unique part of your personality just as the Body Soul has. The Celestial Soul will come to find you in one of your lifetimes here or it may be with you already from the very start of your continued incarnations here on this planet from beyond.

It finds your harmonic signature in the Body Soul (You) that it can most correlate with and which feels most like a perfect match. And so from this moment forward the body Soul and the Celestial Soul energetically integrate and become one with each other. Becoming an integrated Soul that is now on it's way to Self Knowing, Self realization and possibly even Ascension.

As the Celestial Soul comes down at whatever point it does, and integrates with a body spirit of a person incarnate in human form, the Celestial Soul and body spirit within a person start to integrate with together. This is an ancient process that has been happening and occurring continually since the beginnings of humanity. This God Soul Energy which is You, and comes through your senses in the Here and Now inspires the Great Knowing of the Self that is referred to in all of the ancient texts.

This integration level opens the door for definitive levels of elevated Self Knowing that has the potential to bring an individual into a heightened state of creativity and even invention. It also has the power and potential to set the stage and open the gateway for that individual's Soul to move towards a state of ascension, whether while still in human form or at the end of a particular lifetime taking that Soul into a unique state of being.

Ascension is the graduation from the incarnations of the wheel of birth and death. As the energies of the Soul of that person align with the Divine power of the Light, all parts or coinciding spiritual bodies are lifted up or accelerated while the astral body and the Soul, retain the emotional body and the mental body along with the DNA of that person in the current lifetime and is now in suspended animation as that ascended personality. So the person known as you in this lifetime with your personality, emotions, mind and character is lifted into a suspended state of animation.

The normal process at death of the physical body is the release of the physical body while the mental and emotional bodies piggy back with the astral body which is also still housed within the Soul. This version of a person either remains here between worlds for whatever reasons possibly as a guided or moves into the Light and up to the Akashic Records where over a matter of time the mental and emotional selves are absorbed back into the Soul. At that point the personality known as you is known now as just another past lifetime personality in the **Gallery of Akashic Lifetimes.**

So as you can now see there are many dynamics to consider about the Soul and it's cohabitation or enjoinment with your physical body.

As long as we are here at this place in our multi-dimensional viewing of the different perspectives of the Soul's Journey, let's look at a related idea. With all of these ways that the Soul is connected it has great influence in multiple ways. Your Soul and it's vibration is helping to influence the rest of the Soul Group of which you are part. It is also helping to influence or light up the rest of the Soul tree of which your Soul Group is part. It is also lighting up or influencing all of your other lifetimes and all those Souls you are in contact in those life times. You are also influencing or lighting up everyone that you are in contact with in this lifetime in the physical. You are influencing your immediate family as well as the extended ancestral Bloodline.

As you start to shift and become enlightened through personal Self Knowing of studying your own Book of Lives, the energy of your shift moves both forward and back along the time line, past, present and future. it moves also in circular spirals or patterns, broadcasting a beacon of light to other Soul Family Group Members.

So you are a Light to the world and others in so many ways! Even beyond what you once thought. Long ago one of my teachers said that you may walk up to someone at a certain moment in their journey and smile or say something simple and in that moment inspire or changing that individuals's life! So carry on my wayward sons and daughters! Bring your Light out to the rest of the world! We want, need and are waiting for your Light!

Let's talk about Twin Flames which is a subject that everybody wants to know about. It seems that most people want to find out about the concept of a Twin Flame Soul to find that romantic match or that romantic mirror. Not everyone is part of a Twin Flame Soul. This is something you may need to come to grips with.

Let's first look at the concept of twins. Birth twins or identical twins each have their own Body

Spirit. Though they are part of one collaborating or enjoined Celestial Soul. One twin is lighter and more joyful, more easy going, loving and creative, while the other mirrors the other aspects of control, strength and courage. Usually with a stronger personality, more active, and quite different in many ways. Twins can either get along greatly through their total differences or they can agree to disagree.

These two twins are part of the same Soul and when one passes before the other the whole Soul and the other twin in astral body will stay with them. From this dynamic the one twin still in form may exhibit more energy, more creativity, or even more intuition as double the energy is now coming through one person's self and body.

Try to look at this dynamic with a Twin Flame Soul. Two twins which were not born at the same time identically, though which may already be together on the other side of the veil where there is no time and no distance. These two somewhat identical or interlocking Soul counterparts are adrift on the sea of life among all the other Souls. A person may or may not ever meet their twin flame counterpart in a certain life unless it is destined to happen. Sometimes the Twin Flame remains on the other side while one is incarnate. If both parts of the Soul are on the other side at the same time then they are together. If they do not meet in a certain incarnation cycle and yet they are both in human form, they may have agreed previous to incarnating to do some special things in regards to their path, for others or the world.

Meeting your Twin Flame in human form can be a monumental thing. Sometimes it's that exacting perfect fit and you will always be together in a super joyful way. It can also come with the heightened dynamics of both sides of the mirror which we spoke about with identical twins.

Let's talk about Soul Mates. Soul Mates can be friends, family members, lovers, enemies, or even business associates from this life from other lives that you have a great magnetic attraction with. You may have a karmic connection comprised of lessons or Universal cause and effect that needs to be worked out between two soul mates.

Many karmas can be worked out for a person on their own path, though many others require that certain Soul to participate. And again the Guides and Teachers in the higher realms have to plan the timing of your get together with them in order for an exchange of energy to be commenced and cultivated with hopefully favorable results in learning, healing, release, love, admiration and abundance for both Souls. So you can have many Soul Mates to choose from. Sometimes Soul Mate unions are not always as perfect as we would like to see them be, while there is continuously a magnetic connection between both Souls, drawing them together. This is for the sake of karmic connections to be worked out or understood. It does not have to be a great monumental undertaking to complete karma. If the two are able to amicably acknowledge, love and forgive each other with a respectful release the benefits and results can be nothing short of enlightening.

If you are concerned about finding your Twin Flame or Soul mate and that has held you back from connection with someone in a relationship, let me bring you a secret. You do not necessarily or ultimately have to find your Twin Flame or a Soul Mate to have a consciously functioning and loving relationship. It could be that a person you connect with who is not a twin flame or Soul mate can be just as much a great partner and may truly love and support you even more while lifting each other up. This is something to think about. I hope this chapter has been informative and enlightening for you as you are one step closer to your **Ultimate Streaming Moments of Self Knowing.**

YOU HAVE MADE GREAT STRIDES FORWARD IN
YOUR PERSONAL SELF KNOWING AND YOUR SPIRITUAL
QUEST FOR WISDOM.

Chapter 15

LEARNING TO MASTER THE RECORDS & YOUR LIFE

*H*ere we are at the close of the 3rd Book. Or is it just the beginning? We have looked through many different windows to your Soul as well as introspects of your mind and your heart. You have now started to access the core of your lifetimes. You now have a great outline within your knowing that will remain with you throughout this lifetime.

Whether you choose to continue meditating and practicing your entries into your personal Book of Lifetimes and the Akashic Records or you choose to sit with the information for a while and let it run through your being in reference to the rest of your life and world. Whichever way that you choose in approaching the Akashic Records in your life and your practicing of access it will be right for you.

Maybe you are a working practitioner and you would like to use what you have learned to benefit what you are already doing with the people that are coming to you for help. The dynamics of the Akashic Records are integrative by nature. And as you are shown things while working with someone you will get continuous creative insights as you gather insights or info with each person that you are already helping.

In your quest for knowledge and wisdom as you have opened up into this work this is only the beginning. Now you get to put it to work within your life and eventually within the lives of others. This brings to you more experience.

If you take the Akashic Records Center online classes or live workshops and use these books wisely they will serve you well. You will now have more of a natural recall through future life experiences of situations which you cannot explain in the moment. That is when we turn to this material and to the Akashic Records to see what's going on behind the scenes.

You have made great strides forward in your personal Self Knowing and your spiritual quest for wisdom. You now have access to information that is not being taught in the main stream. We hope that in time it will soon come back into the knowing of the group consciousness of humanity. For this knowledge, information and wisdom truly has the potential to shift humanity up to the next level of conscious awareness.

So many things could and would change for the better. You are without a doubt on the road to higher understanding, which will bring you healing of your past lifetimes as well as healing and release and integration of all things in this lifetime. Releasing and embracing those things which have been our stumbling blocks in ways that we never thought we would be able to let go of or rise above.

You are the Love and You are the Light of the Soul that is also part of the Soul of the Universe and of Creator God.

As you tap into greater levels of yourself, your life patterns your thought processes will change whether subtly or dramatically. Doing the Self work which eventually becomes a new way of life is definitely a foundational approach which will always benefit you. Using the Akashic Records to look into why patterns have been recurring for you and understanding that by observing these patterns through past life situations and possibly lost childhood remembrances you stand in the gateway of healing release.

Learning to master the Akashic Records is a process that we are guiding you through with this material. There is everything you need to know as far as the processes, techniques and what can happen and occur for you in your Soul, your ancestry, childhood reflections, your family, your present moments and your future.

You will have the opportunity to start looking at time differently and you will most certainly start to perceive the Soul in new and expanded ways. As you continue to practice accessing the Akashic Records you will be able to navigate your life more clearly. You will start to have a clearer picture of what's going on with most people in society internally and this can help you to have new responses to the world around you.

You will get to say hello to a new world and to a new you! This can be invigorating when for so long you've searched for that magic bullet or that golden chalice to make everything work in your life. Now that you have immersed yourself within this material you have not only a better understanding of the higher dimensions and the other side of the veil, you now have a working model of it and how you as a multi-dimensional being interacts with it. You now have much more to go on than regurgitated spiritual paraphrases that seemingly go nowhere except trailing off into eternity.

This metaphysical approach to your life's experience of your Soul being here on earth is interactive and meant to bring you into a more knowing place withing yourself that gives you foundation and grounding as well as wings at the same time. In order to fly high and to go places within the Universe and higher dimensions that have a meaningful destination, such as the Akashic Records, instead of just escaping out of body, you need a grounded approach to study about the nonphysical in order to have a more unified and expanded approach and experience.

Whimsical meanderings of loosely channelled 'messages' will in the long run not hold water. We need more than just general waxing statements in order to progress spiritually, mentally, emotionally and physically. We require truth statements in a factual form that vibrate the Soul fields and the chakra fields with activating energy therefore waking us up. And we require true elements of the Light in order to do this. Truth, integrity and virtue are your best friends when doing the work within the Records.

If you have had challenges with these aspects in your life, or any other emotional aspects of yourself, not to worry. Looking into the Records through your Soul energy has the power to start realigning you with your Soul energy in ways that will remove inner conflict and move you into a new life within your life. Accessing the Records will help you to re-pattern your thoughts and emotional tendencies, therefore lifting you up and out of recurring or self limiting thoughts, beliefs and patterns in a brand new way.

Patience and virtue are your best friends when accessing your Book of Life and the Akashic Records in general, and don't forget practice, practice, practice. While some of us are naturals at accessing, others need practice to learn the process. Just like painting or playing music. Some of us are natural and some need to learn the creative process and all can benefit from it in our own unique ways. Having to learn from scratch is in no way less than being naturally gifted at something. Both can learn and receive direction in their own unique ways.

Working with the Akashic Records is all about realigning with your Soul at the deepest levels. As this starts to occur, you can heal your body and you can have a great advantage to changing your life. You will start to see things more clearly in many ways and through a new pair of eyes for the first time. As you shift you will see the benefits sometimes right away and sometimes more gradually over time and through positive change, healing and transformation will occur.

I hope that you have enjoyed this study book set and that you will look back and access the information contained here within the material over the course of your lifetime. Life is a journey and a process and much like life, reading the Akashic Records is a process in and of itself. It is all about your life and your lifetimes directly, this is why it is a process and why it is so powerful to help you create a greater, wider, deeper river of knowledge and wisdom which you can draw from. Stop, look and listen often and when life gets interesting or complex, dive into your Book of Life and find out what's truly going on. It will give you knowing, inner peace and the will to move forward and take creative action on your Journey in Life and your Journey Into the Akashic Records.

Bill Foss 1-9-2020

TEACHING TERMS
FOR THE
AKASHIC RECORDS CENTER
CERTIFICATION PROCESS

Akashic Hall of Healing Wisdom - The part of the Akashic Records dedicated specifically to healing and healers available as a place to treat from or as a place of referencing information on any level for an individual's return to wellness.

Akashic Vision Journey Experience - The energetic experience of having your inner vision come on through your eyes and your third eye. Seeing in 3D lucid inner vision which can be momentary or continually streaming. This can be either animated movies or stationary pictures, images, colors or words and/or symbols.

Akashic Light Symbols - A higher dimensional harmonic language of light symbols that are specific to the Akashic Records in frequency. The original symbol language that all Earth/planetary languages and dialects come from. It is possible to read and to translate this language through meditation, visions and writing in order to receive direct messages from the Akasha.

Akashic Shamanic - A form of inquiry and Soul

Healing developed by Bill Foss which employs the dynamics of both the Akashic and Shamanic. Akashic being higher dimensional sky based energy and Shamanic being deep Earth based energy.

Book of Life - Within the Akashic Records each Soul has it's own collection of thought, word and deed responses from every lifetime that it has incarnated in human form. The Book of Life is used by the Soul, and God to guide each individual Soul's purpose, experiences and evolution.

Body Spirit - The part of a person's Soul that more deeply inhabits the physical body, it's organs and it's systems. This part of the Soul carries all of the cellular memories from the current and past lifetimes.

Celestial Soul - This part of the Soul comes from the stars. It can be directly linked to Creator God, the Great Central Sun, or other incarnations in civilizations among the stars prior to earthly incarnations. This part of the Soul carries Divine Intelligence to heal and to connect with it's origins and other Soul family members.

Creative Affirmation Thought Commands Primarily for the used for programming and reprogramming the conscious and the subconscious minds. These are comprised of words, mantras, prayers, affirmations and declarations to the Universe, the external world, and to the self to bring the self into alignment with that which one desires to have in their life experience.

Creative Entanglement - The connections of

a person's Soul to all of the lifetimes. And the connection from the human body to the Soul and into the Records which utilizes the principles of quantum energy as well as past, present, future.

Divine Intelligence - The organic nature of the Universe by which the cosmic process of creation seeks out to permeate and move through all living things. The fabric of the Universe itself is composed and orchestrated by Divine Intelligence. Consciousness unconsciously all pervading throughout all known and yet to be known elements of creation. Communicable with all communicable and noncommunicable beings as Source Light energy.

Divine Timing - Also known as Serendipity or Synchronicity. Those times when the Universe and the teachers, angels, guides and healers working with you on the other side bring into your time and space the perfect timing for protection, healing, manifesting something for you, or meeting a certain individual which you are destined to meet. Often Grace is involved in these situations.

Divine Right - Also known as a person's birthright. Things that would be freely given for you to experience: Joy, Love, Spirituality, Access to your Book of Life, etc.

Divine Universal Law of Free Will - In alignment with your Divine Right, This Universal Law states that no one or no thing has power over you unless you agree or consent to it whether knowingly or unknowingly. Often this happens unknowingly which permits Divine Intervention from another person, spirit, angels, guides or God to remove unwanted interference.

Etheric Wheel of Lifetimes - This is the incarnation cycle and the collection of all of a soul's lifetimes. Often illustrated as a wheel with spokes or connections from each lifetime on the wheel to the Soul as the central hub to all incarnations of lifetimes.

Eternal Now Moment - This is also referred to as the continual streaming of awareness. The continual series of unfolding moments. When you realize that continually you are stepping beyond linear time and space and in direct alignment with Universal Intelligence. Continual focus on the present.

Gallery of Akashic Lifetimes - As a person visits the Akashic Records they will be naturally building a case of all of their past lives. This gallery can be visited or created visually by bringing any and all known past incarnations into one mental room and also announcing an open invitation for any unknown incarnations to reveal themselves by joining this inner Soul circle.

Higher Self - The part of a person's being that is working in the other or higher dimensions. Also known as the Light Body or Angelic Self. Usually depicted by a luminous figure over the physical body.

Inner Child - Each of us has the remembrances of our childhood. As we connect back to this part of ourselves we relive or re-experience emotions, thought patterns and situations. We integrate the Inner Child for the purposes of self healing, release and empowerment in our current life.

Knowing Way of Truth and Light - The original Spiritual light teachings from Atlantis. Also carried forward by Thoth the Atlantean from those times into Egyptian times. Also referred to by Jesus the Christ as the Knowing Way of Truth and Light, the Knowing Way or simply the Way.

Medical Intuitive (or Psychic) Healing - A process of healing involving the use of the healer or practitioner's intuitive abilities, or psychic abilities combined with kinetic energy to move and affect the matter and tissue of the human body in any way that manifests as healing, wellness and wholeness.

Quantum Time Line thee Healing - A healing modality developed by Bill Foss which involves healing of the ancestors, the bloodline and the family tree of an individual. QTLH involves travelling backwards and forwards along the time line simultaneously in order to pin point moments of injury or trauma.

Past, Present & Future Selves - The child self or inner child, the present day self and the higher of perfect God self. Also correlated to the Subconscious, Conscious and Super conscious minds.

Shamanic State of Consciousness - The state of entering into a special Earth dimension reserved and known usually only be those shamans who are involved in the inner trance journeys of soul repair for an individual or group of people. S.S.C. involves travelling to the upper, middle and lower worlds for visionary, learning and healing purposes.

Shamanic Soul Retrieval - The process of healing used by a shaman or shamanic practitioner to bring back lost pieces of a persons Soul energy. Often when Soul energy is missing, taken or becomes lost, a person may operate at a deficit or uneasiness until the missing Soul fragments are returned. Shamanism is an ancient tribal practice of working with the earth's energy and the animal familiars to bring back a person's energy to them and to release anything that has been with them whether elemental energy, another person's energy or a non-physical being which has attached to them for some reason or another.

Soul Timing - This is what is discoverable through studying your Book of Life. Time is overlapping in places and not only a series of linear events. Our Soul has scheduled events to experience which can be altered through spiritual development. Soul Timing is also associated with Divine Timing.

Spatial Reality - The dimensions of reality. If you are to look at reality as the backdrop for your conscious place in the world, you are operating physically in a world as your senses project out into the time and dimensional space of spatial reality.

(Live) Streaming Akashic Vision - This occurs when you are fully engaged in your visual Akashic Records practice and there is a direct connection between the Records and your Soul energy streaming down into your mind's eye, your senses, you physical and energy bodies and your chakras. It becomes a very vivid and colorful full streaming high definition experience.

Tapestry of Souls - Within the Akashic Records a great monogram moving with energy and color which is a living diagram of all Souls incarnate on the planet and the Soul groups. A holographic mural important to all life itself.

Quantum Universal Space Time Reality - This could also be explained as the Eternal Now Moment. The expanded version is a template of overlaying time lines and realities. Parallel realities and alternate realities cascading outside of our continuing reality. These versions of time contain different variations of what we're experiencing in this reality. Some similar and some very different versions. Influenced by thought energy and when not played out in this reality, sent into an alternate reality. Beyond linear time and that which linear time is part of.

Universal Expansion of Cosmic Oneness - Your personal energy within and your energy fields have a tendency to expand and contract in reaction and response to life. As you become more expanded continually your fields will naturally start to flow and expand with more rhythmic tides of expansion and contraction. As expansion continues your energy body will adjust and arrive at a more relaxed balance between the previous levels of guarded contraction and new levels of what we call Universal Expansion.

Ultimate Streaming Moments of Self Knowing- These are the moments that you could write novels about. Very rich with the inner informations, thoughts and feelings made possible by the co-participation with Divine Intelligence. These are the defining special moments in one's life when a pinnacle of self perception or self realization is achieved. We often spiritually work towards this state though the masters often say that we eventually allow it to happen.

GLOSSARY

Akashic Records - A sanskrit term meaning sky, space or ether. A living energetic library of every past, present, future moments of every person, place or thing, animate and inanimate. Used by God and our Souls to determine the advancement, healing and karma of the lifetimes lived.

Akashic Vision - The energetic inner visionary pictures, visions and movies that are experienced during Akashic Records, readings, practices and journeys. Akashic Vision can be dream like bringing intermittent dream like images to very lucid soul frequency movies which are interactive and can stream energy into a person through the interaction with the experience.

Alternate Realities - A universe hypothesized in some cosmological models to exist along with our own universe, possibly obeying different physical laws and having the potential for the transfer of information between universes.

Ascension - The rise of the *'Christ-consciousness'* in mankind to the point that the individual is beyond the powers of reincarnation and karma. The word *'resurrection'* as found in the New Testament is best translated as 'ascension'. After millennia of reincarnation, the soul finally gets off the wheel of karma in *'ascension'*. The transformation of a person's current ego with the light body into an ascended state of existence being able to move between dimensions including the earth plane.

Asana - A body position, typically associated with the practice of Yoga, originally identified as a mastery of sitting still. In the context of Yoga practice, asana refers to two things: the place where a practitioner (or yogin, in general usage), yogi (male), or yogini (female) sits and the manner (posture) in which he/ she sits. In the Yoga sutras, Patanjali suggests that asana is "to be seated in a position that is firm, but relaxed" for extended, or timeless periods.

As a repertoire of postures were promoted to exercise the body-mind over the centuries to the present day, when yoga is sought as a primarily physical exercise form, modern usage has come to include variations from lying on the back and standing on the head, to a variety of other positions. However, in the Yoga sutras, Patanjali mentions the execution of sitting with a steadfast mind for extended periods as the third of the eight limbs of Classical or Raja yoga,but does not reference standing postures or kriyās.

Yoga practitioners (even those who are adepts at various complex postures) who seek the "simple" practice of chair-less sitting generally find it impossible or surprisingly grueling to sit still for the traditional minimum of one hour (as still practiced in eastern Vipassana), some of them then dedicating their practice to sitting asana and the sensations and mind-states that arise and evaporate in extended sits.

Ascended Masters - Spiritually enlightened beings who in past incarnations were ordinary humans, but who have undergone a series of spiritual transformations. The Ascended Master Teachings refer to the Sixth Initiation as Ascension. According to the Ascended Master Teachings, a 'Master' (or 'Spiritual Master') is a human being who has taken the Fifth Initiation and is thereby capable of dwelling on the 5th dimension. An 'Ascended Master' is a human being who has taken the Sixth Initiation and is thereby capable of dwelling on the 6th dimension. An 'Ascended Master' is a human being who has regained full union with his 'I AM Presence.' When a human being has regained full union with his 'I AM Presence,' that state of full union is referred to as 'Ascension' Technically, a human being 'ascends' when he takes the Sixth Initiation.

Astral Plane -   The 5th Dimension. The 'other-wordly' plane of existence closest to the 3D physical reality. This dimension acts as a go-tween for all of the many souls, spirits and entities interacting with humans or going on to experience other worlds. Also associated with psychic activity.

Awareness - having knowledge or perception of a situation or fact. Concerned and well-informed about a particular situation or development.

Ayurvedic - the traditional Hindu system of medicine, which is based on the idea of balance in bodily systems and uses diet, herbal treatment, and yogic breathing. Based around the principles of the elements: Earth, Water, Fire, Wood, Air. From Sanskrit āyus 'life' + veda 'science.'

Bhoddisatva - in Buddhism one who has attained prajna, or Enlightenment, but who postpones Nirvana in order to help others to attain Enlightenment.

Brain Waves:

Beta waves (38 - 15 Hz) - Are the brainwaves of our "normal" waking consciousness, of our outward attention, of logical, conscious and analytical thinking. High frequency beta ("splayed beta") is seen with restlessness, stress, anxiety, panic or while our inner critic or commentator is active. Splayed beta can be differentiated from the low frequency beta of the awakened mind, when thinking feels clear, alert, creative and to the point.

Alpha brainwaves (14 - 8 Hz) are seen when we are in a relaxed state, daydreaming or visualizing ("sensualising" seems to be more appropriate as imagination in all senses - hearing, kinesthetic, smell, taste etc. - stimulates alpha waves. Your visual sense may not necessarily be the strongest for you. Some people rather feel an inner knowing). We need alpha waves as the bridge to the lower frequencies of the subconscious (theta), if we want to remember the content of our dreams or our meditation, or if we want to retrieve information from our subconscious. For this reason alpha is especially important in combination with other brainwaves.

Theta brainwaves (7 - 4 Hz) Represents the subconscious. We see theta during dream sleep (REM sleep), meditation, during peak experiences and creative states. In theta we find unconscious or suppressed parts of our psyche as well as our creativity and spirituality. Theta images are usually less distinct and colorful than alpha images, sometimes of a blueish color, but they often feel more profound and meaningful. As long as we only produce theta brainwaves, their content will stay inaccessible to our waking mind. We need alpha to bridge the gap between theta and beta brainwaves to consciously experience or remember theta content.

Delta brainwaves (3 - 0.5 Hz) Are the brainwaves of the lowest frequency and represent the unconscious. If we only produce delta we will find us in dreamless deep sleep, but we also see delta in various combinations with other brainwaves. They may then represent intuition, curiosity, a kind of radar, hunches or a "feeling" for situations and other people. Delta is often seen with people who work in therapeutic environments or professions and with people who have had traumatic experiences and have developed a "radar" for difficult situations.

Gamma brainwaves (100 - 38 Hz) were detected later than the other brainwaves, less is known about them so far. They have been seen in states of peak performance (both physical and mental), high focus and concentration and during mystic and transcendental experiences. A lot of research is currently being done on gamma brainwaves in the 40 Hz range during meditation. One of the characteristics of gamma waves is a synchronisation of activity over wide areas of the brain. Gamma brainwaves are not easy to detect because of their low amplitude and can only partly be displayed on the Mind Mirror screen. Sometimes they may be seen as a narrow frequency band at 38 Hz.

Buddhism - A religion and philosophy indigenous to the Indian subcontinent and encompasses a variety of traditions, beliefs, and practices largely based on teachings attributed to Siddhartha Gautama, who is commonly known as the Buddha (meaning *'the awakened one'* in Sanskrit and Pāli). The Buddha lived and taught in the eastern part of Indian subcontinent some time between the 6th and 4th centuries BCE. He is recognized by Buddhists as an awakened or enlightened teacher who shared his insights to help sentient beings end suffering through eliminating ignorance, craving, and hatred, by way of understanding and seeing dependent origination and no-self, and thus attain the highest happiness, nirvana. The originating teacher of Vipassana.

Bloodline - Direct line of descent; pedigree. Your ancestors, relatives and heritage.

Chakra - (in Eastern thought) each of the centers of spiritual power in the human body, seven in number along the spine from tailbone to crown of the head. From Sanskrit chakra *'wheel or circle'*.

Chi (also ki,ka) The vital force believed in Taoism and other Chinese doctrines, spiritual and religious practices, thought to be inherent in all things. The unimpeded circulation of chi and a balance of its negative and positive forms in the body are held to be essential to good health in traditional Chinese medicine. Literal translation: energy. Also known as ki (*Japanese*) and ka (*Egyptian*)

Clairaudience - (*French - clair meaning 'clear' and audience meaning "hearing"*) A form of clairvoyant extra-sensory perception in which a person acquires information by paranormal auditory means. The ability to hear in a paranormal manner. May refer not to actual perception of sound, but may instead indicate impressions of the "inner mental ear" or "*the 3rd ear*". Perception of sounds, voices, tones, or noises which are not normally audible. A clairaudient (person) might hear the voices or thoughts of the spirits, messages from God, angels, masters, gurus, or persons who are discarnate, or on the other side.

Clairsentience - (*French - clair meaning 'clear'and 'sentience' is derived from the Latin sentire,'to feel'*) A form of clairvoyant extra-sensory perception wherein a person acquires psychic knowledge by feeling. One of the six special human functions mentioned in Buddhism. Refers to a person who can feel the vibration of other people. There are many different degrees of clairsentience ranging from the perception of diseases or sickness of other people (*aka medical intuitive*) to the thoughts or emotions of other people. It differs from third eye activity in that instead of vivid pictures in the mind, a very vivid feeling can form. Psychometry is related to clairsentience.(*Psyche and metric, which means 'soul-measuring'*).

Clairvoyance - (*French - clair meaning 'clear' and voyance meaning 'vision'*) is used to refer to the ability to gain information about an object, person, location or physical event through means other than the known human senses, a form of extra-sensory perception (E.S.P.). A person said to have the ability of clairvoyance is referred to as a clairvoyant -'*one who sees clearly*'.

Consciousness - The quality or state of being aware especially within ones self. A sense of one's personal or collective identity, including the attitudes, beliefs, and sensitivities held by or considered characteristic of an individual or group. Totality of conscious states of an individual.

De ja vu - *(French - literally 'already seen')* is the impression that one has already witnessed or experienced a current situation, even though the exact circumstances of the prior encounter are unclear and were perhaps imagined. The term was coined by a French psychic researcher, Émile Boirac (1851–1917) in his book L'Avenir des sciences psychiques ('The Future of Psychic Sciences')

Deities - A being, natural, supernatural or preternatural, with superhuman powers or qualities, and who may be thought of as holy, divine, or sacred. Believers consider that they can communicate with the deity, who can respond supernaturally to their entreaties. Deities are depicted in a variety of forms, but are also frequently expressed as having human form. Deities are often thought to be immortal, and are commonly assumed to have personalities and to possess consciousness, intellects, desires, and emotions comparable but usually superior to those of humans.

Divination - (from Latin divinare *'to foresee, to be inspired by a god'*, related to divinus, divine) is the attempt to gain insight into a question or situation by way of an occultic standardized process or ritual. Used in various forms for thousands of years, diviners ascertain their interpretations of how a querent should proceed by reading signs, events, or omens, or through alleged contact with a supernatural agency. Divination can be seen as a systematic method with which to organize what appear to be disjointed, random facets of existence such that they provide insight into a problem at hand. If a distinction is to be made between divination and fortune-telling, divination has a formal or ritual and often social character, usually in a religious context, as seen in traditional African medicine; while fortune-telling is a more everyday practice for personal purposes. Particular divination methods vary by culture and religion.

DNA - *Deoxyribonucleic Acid* is a nucleic acid containing the genetic instructions used in the development and functioning of all known living organisms (with the exception of RNA viruses). The DNA segments carrying this genetic information are called genes. Likewise, other DNA sequences have structural purposes, or are involved in regulating the use of this genetic information. Along with RNA and proteins, DNA is one of the three major macromolecules that are essential for all known forms of life.

Ego - A person's sense of self-esteem or self-importance: a boost to my ego. Psychoanalysis the part of the mind that mediates between the conscious and the unconscious and is responsible for reality testing and a sense of personal identity.

Elohim - A group of special or higher order of angels who are in charge of utilizing the creation forces of the Light of Creator God. Known also to to work with the Council of Twelve and as guardians of the Akashic Records.

Empathy or Empathic ability - The action of understanding, being aware of, being sensitive to, and vicariously experiencing the feelings, thoughts, and experience of another in either the past or present time line without previously having those feelings, thoughts, and experience fully communicated in an objectively explicit manner about the person, feelings, or situation. Someone known to use empathic abilities may be referred to as an 'empath'.

Enlightenment - Spiritual revelation or deep insight into the meaning and purpose of all things, communication with or understanding of the mind of God, profound spiritual understanding or a fundamentally changed consciousness whereby everything is perceived as a unity. Freedom from desire and other worldly passions. For Hindus, as for Buddhists and Jains, enlightenment ends the cycle of reincarnation. Souls are held to enter many different bodies through the course of their existence. In each of the lives they lead they develop spiritually. Enlightenment is a state of freedom from the ignorance that causes suffering.

E.S.P. (Extra Sensory Perception) - Psychic abilities including but not limited to: mind reading, future sight, second sight, de ja vu, remote viewing, etc. Involving the acquisition or effect of past, present or future information that cannot be deduced from presently available and normally acquired sense-based information or laws of physics and / or nature.

Etherioplasma - the term is a combination of ether (the invisible energy that carries the human spirit that survives each death to form a new physical body) and the plasma energy that transfers the subtle electromagnetic forces from the soul to the human form that the human spirit use to help animate the human form. Etherio – plasmic. The actual measureable yet invisible energy substance of the Soul.

Familiars - Familiar spirits *(sometimes referred to simply as 'familiars')* were supernatural entities believed to assist witches and cunning folk in their practice of magic. According to folklore, they would appear in numerous guises, often as an animal, but also at times as a human or humanoid figure, and were described as *"clearly defined, three-dimensional... forms, vivid with color and animated with movement and sound"* by those alleging to have come into contact with them, unlike later descriptions of ghosts with their "smoky, undefined forms. Also referred to as Animal spirits who work with Shamans of different cultures as well as in Native American spiritualism.

Flower of Life - The Flower of Life is a name for

a geometrical figure composed of multiple evenly-spaced, overlapping circles. This figure, used as a decorative motif since ancient times, forms a flower-like pattern with the symmetrical structure of a hexagon. A "Flower of Life" figure consists of seven or more overlapping circles, in which the center of each circle is on the circumference of up to six surrounding circles of the same diameter. However, the surrounding circles need not be clearly or completely drawn; in fact, some ancient symbols that are claimed as examples of the Flower of Life contain only a single circle or hexagon.

Grace - It has been defined as the divine influence which operates in humans to regenerate and sanctify, to inspire virtuous impulses, and to impart strength to endure trial and resist temptation and as an individual virtue or excellence of divine origin. It can also be perceived as divine intervention, blessings that were not asked for or even undeserved blessings.

Gregorian Time - The system of dates used by most of the world. The Gregorian calendar was proposed by the Calabrian doctor Aloysius Lilius and was decreed by, and named after, Pope Gregory XIII on 1582-02-24. It corrected the Julian calendar whose years were slightly longer than the solar year. It also replaced the lunar calendar which was also out of time with the seasons.

The correction was achieved by skipping several days as a one-off re-synchronization and then dropping three leap days every 400 hundred years.

In the revised system, leap years are all years divisible by 4 but excluding those divisible by 100 but including those divisible by 400. This gives a mean calendar year of 365.2425 days = 52.1775 weeks = 8,765.82 hours = 525,949.2 minutes = 31,556,952 seconds. Leap seconds are occasionally added to this to correct for irregularities in the Earth's rotation.

Guardian Angels - An angel assigned to protect and guide a particular person or group. The appearance of guardian angels can be traced throughout all antiquity. The concept of tutelary angels and their hierarchy was extensively developed in Christianity in the 5th century by Pseudo - Dionysius the Areopagite.

Guru - a Sanskrit term for *'teacher'* or *'master'*, especially in Eastern or Indian religions. The Hindu guru - shishya tradition is the oral tradition or religious doctrine transmitted from teacher to student. A teacher and guide in spiritual and philosophical matters. A trusted counselor and adviser; a mentor. A personal spiritual teacher.

Hatha Yoga - Traditional hatha yoga is a holistic yogic path, including disciplines, postures (asana), purification procedures (shatkriya), gestures (mudra), breathing (pranayama), and meditation. The hatha yoga predominantly practiced in the West consists of mostly asanas understood as physical exercises. It is also recognized as a stress-reducing practice.

Hinduism - The predominant religion of the Indian subcontinent, and one of its indigenous religions.

Among other practices and philosophies, Hinduism includes a wide spectrum of laws and prescriptions of *'daily morality'* based on the notion of karma, dharma, and societal norms. Hinduism is a conglomeration of distinct intellectual or philosophical points of view, rather than a rigid common set of beliefs. Hinduism is formed of diverse traditions and has no single founder. Among its direct roots is the historical Vedic religion of Iron Age India and, as such, Hinduism is often called the *'oldest living major religion'* in the world.

I Am That I Am or Holy I Am Presence - The Self begins with that which is the permanent atom of being and the cause out of which the effect proceeds. We call this cause the I AM THAT I AM, the Presence of the I AM, or the I AM Presence.

I find that God by any name can be reduced to this sense of the eternal Presence. It defines being, and I see it as a sphere of intense light that marks the point of my origin. It is the permanent part of me, of which I am very aware, and the point to which I will return at the conclusion of this life.

Incarnation - literally means embodied in flesh or taking on flesh. It refers to the conception and birth of a sentient creature (generally a human) who is the material manifestation of a soul, entity, god or God, whose original nature is non-physical. In its religious context the word is used to mean the descent from Heaven of a god, or divine being in human/animal form on Earth.

Introspection - (or internal perception) Is the

self-examination of one's conscious thoughts and feelings. The process of introspection relies exclusively on the purposeful and rational self-observation of one's mental, physical, emotional and spiritual state; however, introspection is sometimes referenced in a spiritual context as the examination of one's soul. Introspection is the act of human self-reflection, and opposite to external observation.

Intuition - The ability to understand something immediately, without the need for conscious reasoning. The ability to acquire knowledge without the use of reason. The act or faculty of knowing or sensing without the use of rational processes; immediate cognition The word 'intuition' comes from the Latin word *'intueri'*, which is often roughly translated as meaning *'to look inside''* or *'to contemplate'*. Intuition may provide us with information that we cannot justify by ordinary means.

Disincarnate - Having no material body or form. Souls who are between lifetimes of incarnation. Unchanging, eternal, and mysterious Ein Sof (no end)

Karma - *Pali: kamma* means action, work or deed; it also refers to the principle of causality where intent and actions of an individual influence the future of that individual. Good intent and good deed contribute to good karma and future happiness, while bad intent and bad deed contribute to bad karma and future suffering. Karma is closely associated with the idea of rebirth in some schools of Asian religions. In these schools, karma in the present affects one's future in the current life, as well as the nature and quality of future lives - or, one's saṃsāra. In Hinduism & Buddhism, The total effect of a person's actions and conduct during the successive phases of the person's existence, regarded as determining the person's destiny. Once karmas are experienced and repaid, one may leave the cycle of reincarnation. Related to cause and effect and the law of attraction.

Kriya Yoga - Described by its practitioners as the ancient Yoga system revived in modern times by Mahavatar Babaji through his disciple Lahiri Mahasaya, circa 1861, and brought into popular awareness through Paramahansa Yogananda's book *'Autobiography of a Yogi'*. The system consists of a number of levels of Pranayama based on techniques that are intended to rapidly accelerate spiritual development and engender a profound state of tranquility and God-communion The term Kriya Yoga was developed in North India from an ancient tradition. The root of the Sanskrit word literally means *'to do'* and a true 'Kriya' technique always involves work with the body and the mind simultaneously. Kriya is a form of meditation involving Tantric Shakti flow of subtle energy within the practitioner's mind & body.

Kundalini - Described as a sleeping, dormant potential force in the human organism. It is one of the components of an esoteric description of the 'subtle body', which consists of nadis (energy channels), chakras (psychic centres), prana (subtle energy), and bindu (drops of essence). Kundalini is described as being coiled up at the base of the spine, usually within muladhara (base) chakra. The image given is that of a serpent coiled three and a half times around a smokey grey lingam. Each coil is said to represent one of the three gunas, with the half coil signifying transcendence. Through meditation, and various esoteric practices, such as Kundalini Yoga, Sahaja Yoga, and Kriya Yoga, the kundalini is awakened, and can rise up through the central nadi, called sushumna, that rises up inside or alongside the spine in the spinal fluid. The progress of kundalini through the different chakras leads to different levels of awakening and mystical experience, until the kundalini finally reaches the top of the head, Sahasrara chakra, producing an extremely profound mystical experience that is said to be indescribable.

Knowing Way of Truth and Light - The original Christ teachings which came from Atlantis. Also known as the Way Teachings, The Way, The Knowing Way.

Love- An emotion of a strong affection and personal attachment. Love is also a virtue representing all of human kindness, compassion, and affection - The unselfish loyal and benevolent concern for the good of another. Love may describe actions towards others or oneself based on compassion or affection. Love refers to a variety of different feelings, states, and attitudes, ranging from pleasure

(*"I loved that meal"*) to interpersonal attraction (*"I love my partner"*). 'Love' may refer specifically to the passionate desire and intimacy of romantic love, to the sexual love of eros, to the emotional closeness of family love, to the platonic love that defines friendship, or to the profound oneness or devotion of religious love, or to a concept of love that encompasses all of those feelings. This diversity of uses and meanings, combined with the complexity of the feelings involved, makes love unusually difficult to consistently define, compared to other emotional states. Love in its various forms acts as a major facilitator of interpersonal relationships and, owing to its central psychological importance, is one of the most common themes in the creative arts.

Lymph (glands) - Physiology a colorless fluid containing white blood cells, that bathes the tissues and drains through the lymphatic system into the bloodstream. Fluid exuding from a sore or inflamed tissue. Literary pure water.

Mala - A string of beads worn around the neck or wrist, traditionally of 108 bead count, to be used for prayers, mantras and chants. From the ancient Eastern traditions, and can also refer to a catholic rosary.

Mandala - A Sanskrit word meaning *'circle.'* In the Buddhist and Hindu religious traditions sacred art often takes a mandala form. The basic form of most Hindu and Buddhist mandalas is a square with four gates containing a circle with a center point. Each gate is in the shape of a T. Mandalas often exhibit radial balance. These mandalas, concentric diagrams, have spiritual and ritual significance in both Buddhism and Hinduism.

The term is of Hindu origin and appears in the Rig Veda as the name of the sections of the work, but is also used in other Indian religions, particularly Buddhism. In the Tibetan branch of Vajrayana Buddhism, mandalas have been developed into sand painting. They are also a key part of anuttara yoga tantra meditation practices. In various spiritual traditions, mandalas may be employed for focusing attention of aspirants and adepts, as a spiritual teaching tool, for establishing a sacred space, and as an aid to meditation and trance induction. It's symbolic nature can help one "to access progressively deeper levels of the unconscious, ultimately assisting the meditator to experience a mystical sense of oneness with the ultimate unity from which the cosmos in all its manifold forms arises." The psychoanalyst Carl Jung saw the mandala as *"a representation of the unconscious self,"* and believed his paintings of mandalas enabled him to identify emotional disorders and work towards wholeness in personality.

Mantras - a sound, seed sound, syllable, word, or group of words that is considered capable of creating (spiritual) transformation when used as a written or chanted prayer. A sacred verbal formula repeated in prayer, meditation, or incantation, such as an invocation of God, a magic spell, or a syllable or portion of scripture containing mystical potentialities. Chanted individually and in groups both silently and aloud traditionally 108 times and with the use of a mala or prayer beads.

Mediumship - Involves a cooperating effort between a person on the Earth plane (the medium or channel) and a person in Spirit (the communicator).

Mudras - In Sanskrit: *'seal'*, *'mark'*, or *'gesture'*; Tibetan, *chakgya* is a symbolic or ritual gesture in Hinduism and Buddhism. While some mudrās involve the entire body, most are performed with the hands and fingers. A mudrā is a spiritual gesture and an energetic seal of authenticity employed in the iconography and spiritual practice of Indian religions and traditions of Dharma and Taoism. One hundred and eight mudras are used in regular Tantric rituals. In yoga, mudrās are used in conjunction with pranayama (yogic breathing exercises), generally while seated in Padmasana, Sukhasana or Vajrasana pose, to stimulate different parts of the body involved with breathing and to affect the flow of prana in the body.

Meditation - A practice in which an individual trains the mind or induces a mode of consciousness, either to realize some benefit or as an end in itself. The term meditation refers to a broad variety of practices (much like the term sports) that includes techniques designed to promote relaxation, build internal energy or life force (qi, ki, prana, etc.) and develop compassion, love, patience, generosity and forgiveness. A particularly ambitious form of meditation aims at effortlessly sustained single-pointed concentration single-pointed analysis, meant to enable its practitioner to enjoy an indestructible sense of well-being while engaging in any life activity.

Metatron's Cube - The name of Metatron's Cube makes reference to Metatron, an angel mentioned in apocryphal texts including the Second Book of Enoch and the Book of the Palaces. These texts rank Metatron second only to the Abrahamic God in the hierarchy of spiritual beings. The derivation of Metatron's cube from the tree of life, which the Talmud clearly states was excluded from human experience during the exile from Eden.

Metatron's cube contains every shape that exists in the universe God has created, and those shapes are the building blocks of all physical matter, which are known as Platonic solids (because the philosopher Plato linked them to the spirit world of heaven and the physical elements on Earth).

The pattern delineated by many of the lines can be created by orthographic projections of the first three Platonic solids. Specifically, the line pattern includes projections of a double tetrahedron (aka stellated octahedron), a cube within a cube (a three-dimensional projection of a tesseract), and an octahedron.

Monad - Was a term for Divinity or the first being, or the totality of all beings. Monad being the source or the One meaning without division.

Mysticism - from the Greek, mystikos, meaning 'an initiate') is the knowledge of, and especially the personal experience of, states of consciousness, or levels of being, or aspects of reality, beyond normal human perception, including experience of and even communion with a supreme being.

Neocortex - The neocortex consists of the grey matter, or neuronal cell bodies and unmyelinated fibers, surrounding the deeper white matter (myelinated axons) in the cerebrum. The neocortex is smooth in rodents and other small mammals, whereas in primates and other larger mammals it has deep grooves (sulci) and wrinkles (gyri). These folds allow the surface area of the neocortex to increase far beyond what could otherwise be fit in the same size skull. All human brains have the same overall pattern of main gyri and sulci, although they differ in detail from one person to another. The mechanism by which the gyri form during embryogenesis is not entirely clear. However, it may be due to differences in cellular proliferation rates in different areas of the cortex early in embryonic development.

Om or Aum - is a mystical sound of Sanskrit origin, sacred and important in various Dharmic religions such as Hinduism, Buddhism, and Jainism. It is placed at the beginning of most Hindu texts as a sacred incantation to be intoned at the beginning and end of a reading of the Vedas or prior to any prayer or mantra. It is used at the end of the invocation to the god being sacrificed to (anuvakya) as an invitation to and for that God to partake of the sacrifice. The Māndukya Upanishad is entirely devoted to the explanation of the syllable. The syllable consists of three phonemes, a (Vaishvanara), u (Hiranyagarbha), and m(Ishvara), which symbolize the beginning, duration, and dissolution of the universe and the associated gods Brahma, Vishnu, and Shiva, respectively. The name omkara is taken as a name of God in the Hindu revivalist Arya Samaj and can be translated as *"I Am Existence"*. Also referred to as the primordial vibrational tone behind all realities and dimensions. Monks and Siddhas have reported to hear this tone vibrating in the deepest levels of trance and meditation.

Om Mani Padme Hum - *"The jewel of consciousness is in the lotus of my heart"* and *"I bow to the light within"* are meditative translations to focus upon while using this mantra. Om coincides with the 3rd eye and forehead, Mani - back of the head, Padme - heart and Hum - throat. Visualizing a ring of God's Divine light through these centers while chanting this mantra clears away negativity, pain, fear and stress and brings compassion and healing to the heart, mind and body, while opening and blending what the higher teachings refer to as the Heart/Mind. Tibetan Buddhists believe that saying this mantra (prayer), Om Mani Padme Hum, out loud or silently to oneself, invokes the powerful benevolent attention and blessings of Chenrezig, the embodiment of compassion. Viewing the written form of the mantra is said to have the same effect. It is said that all the teachings of the Buddha are contained in this mantra.

According to the Dali Lama: "It is very good to recite the mantra **Om Mani Padme Hum**, but while you are doing it, you should be thinking on it's meaning, for the meaning of the six syllables is great and vast... The first, '*Om*' symbolizes the practitioner's impure body, speech, and mind; it also symbolizes the pure exalted body, speech, and mind of a Buddha. The path is indicated by the next four syllables. '*Mani*', meaning jewel, symbolizes the factors of method: (the) altruistic intention to become enlightened, compassion, and love. The two syllables, '*Padme*', meaning lotus, symbolize wisdom. Purity must be achieved by an indivisible unity of method and wisdom, symbolized by the final syllable '*Hum*', which indicates indivisibility. Thus the six syllables, '*Om Mani Padme Hum*', mean that in dependence on the practice of a path which is an indivisible union of method and wisdom, you can transform your impure body, speech, and mind into the pure exalted body, speech, and mind of a Buddha"

Omnipresence - The property of being present everywhere. This characteristic is most commonly used in a religious context, as most doctrines bestow the trait of omnipresence onto a superior, a deity or God. This also identifies the universe and divinity; in divine omnipresence, the divine and universe are separate, but the divine is present everywhere.

Hinduism, and other religions that derive from it, incorporate the theory of transcendent and immanent omnipresence which is the traditional meaning of the word, Brahman. This theory defines a universal and fundamental substance, which is the source of all physical existence. Divine omnipresence is thus one of the divine attributes.

Past Lives - According to the study of reincarnation, the lives that our soul has previously lived or participated in. Past lives can be incarnations within the same family or within different races and regions of the world. These past lives are often discoverable through dreams, past life regression, Shamanic Journeys and Journeys into the Akashic Records and a person's Book of Lifetimes.

Pan Fairy Realm - The 2nd Dimensional beings that often interact with nature. Fairies, gnomes, earth and nature devas that assist mother earth in tending her planetary garden. Intermittently these being can find their way into human incarnation by way of evolution. Often these folks can feel a deep bond with mother nature without knowing why. Some incarnate knowing where they came from.

Pineal Gland - (or the *'third eye'*) is a small endocrine gland in the brain. It produces the serotonin derivative melatonin, a hormone that affects the modulation of wake/sleep patterns and seasonal functions. Its shape resembles a tiny pine cone (hence its name), and it is located near the centre of the brain, between the two hemispheres, tucked in a groove where the two rounded thalamic bodies join. The Pineal Gland has for long been associated with Esoteric Knowledge surrounding the spiritual, metaphysical aspects of consciousness and the self. René Descartes, who dedicated much time to the study of the pineal gland, called it the 'Seat of the Soul'. He believed that it was the point of connection between the intellect and the body.

Directly behind the root of the nose (3rd eye chakra) floating in a small lake of cerebrospinal fluid. It is our body's biological clock. The pineal gland has been supplied with the best blood, oxygen and nutrient mix available other than that received by our kidneys. It acts as a receiving mechanism capable of monitoring electro-magnetic fields and helping align bodies in space. With its central hormone, Melatonin, the pineal not only regulates sleep/wake cycles and the aging process, but also appears to act as the Mistress Gland (sofia)* orchestrating the body's entire endocrine system and thus, energetically speaking, the chakra system. It is also responsible for shamanic states, visions, kundalini awakening e.t.c.

Pituitary Gland - An endocrine gland about the size of a pea and weighing 0.5 grams (0.018 oz) in humans. It is not a part of the brain. It is a protrusion off the bottom of the hypothalamus at the base of the brain, and rests in a small, bony cavity (sella turcica) covered by a dural fold (diaphragma sellae). The pituitary is functionally connected to the hypothalamus by the median eminence via a small tube called the infundibular stem (Pituitary stalk). The pituitary fossa, in which the pituitary gland sits, is situated in the sphenoid bone in the middle cranial fossa at the base of the brain.

The pituitary gland secretes nine hormones that regulate homeostasis. The Pituitary Gland is known as the Master Gland of the Endocrine System. It's secretions regulate all the other Endocrine Glands. This gland represents one's ability to coordinate the different aspects of one's Life. Problems represent difficulty doing this. The Pituitary Gland is linked to the Hypothalamus, also located in the brain, whose function is to maintain Homeostasis in the body. That is the body's tendency to return automatically to its level of highest functioning. Metaphysically, this means aligning the frequencies of the physical and energetic bodies to homeostatically return to one's highest spiritual functioning. The pituitary gland is called the *"Seat of the Mind"* with the frontal lobe regulating emotional thoughts such as poetry and music, and the anterior lobe regulating concrete thought and intellectual concepts. The pineal gland is known as the *'Seat of Illumination, Intuition and Cosmic Consciousness'*. The pineal gland is to the pituitary gland what intuition is to reason. The glandular system also coincides with the chakra system.

Prana - The Sanskrit word for *'vital life'* (from the root prā 'to fill',). It is one of the five organs of vitality or sensation, prana *"breath"*, vac *'speech'*, chakshus *'sight'*, shrotra *'hearing'*, and manas *'thought'* (nose, mouth, eyes, ears and mind). In Vedantic philosophy, prana is the notion of a vital, life-sustaining force of living beings and vital energy, comparable to the Chinese notion of Qi. Prana is a central concept in Hinduism, particularly in Ayurveda and Yoga. It flows through a network of fine subtle channels called nadis. Its most subtle material form is the breath, but it is also to be found in the blood, and its most concentrated form is semen in men and vaginal fluid in women. Prana was first expounded in the Upanishads, where it is part of the worldly, physical realm, sustaining the body and the mother of thought and thus also of the mind. Prana suffuses all living forms but is not itself the Atman or individual soul. In the Ayurveda, the Sun and sunshine are held to be a source of prana.

Pranayama - A Sanskrit word meaning 'extension of the prana or breath' or more accurately, *'extension of the life force'*. The word is composed of two Sanskrit words, Prāna, life force, or vital energy, particularly, the breath, and 'ayāma', to extend or draw out.

Psyche - The totality of the human mind, conscious, and unconscious. Psychology is the scientific or objective study of the psyche. The word has a long history of use in psychology and philosophy, dating back to ancient times, and has been one of the fundamental concepts for understanding human nature from a scientific point of view.

Psychic - Relating to or denoting faculties or phenomena that are apparently inexplicable by natural laws, especially involving telepathy or clairvoyance: psychic powers. A person appearing or considered to have powers of telepathy or clairvoyance. Of or relating to the soul or mind. From the Greek psychikos—'*of the mind, mental*', is a person who possesses an ability to perceive information hidden from the normal senses through extrasensory perception (ESP), It can also denote an ability of the mind to influence the world physically using psychokinetic powers.

Elaborate systems of divination and fortune - telling date back to ancient times. Perhaps the most widely-known system of early civilization fortune - telling was astrology, where practitioners believed the relative positions of celestial bodies could lend insight into people's lives and even predict their future circumstances. Some fortune-tellers were said to be able to make predictions without the use of ritualistic objects or special, spiritual, or energy tools for diving information. More so through direct apprehension or vision of the past, present or future. These people were known as seers or prophets, and in later times as clairvoyants and psychics.

Psychic Surgery - Psychic Surgeons are gifted healers that have been blessed with the ability to completely melt or remove cysts, tumors, calcium deposits, pus, energy blockages, etc.. from the body using their bare hands. They can also help with other serious diseases from the heart, liver, adrenal, thyroid, etc..

Qi Gong - a practice of aligning breath, movement, and awareness for exercise, healing, and meditation. With roots in Chinese medicine, martial arts, and philosophy, qigong is traditionally viewed as a practice to cultivate and balance qi (chi) or what has been translated as *'intrinsic life energy'*. Typically a Qigong practice involves rhythmic breathing coordinated with slow stylized repetition of fluid movement, a calm mindful state, and visualization of guiding qi through the body. Qigong is now practiced throughout China and worldwide, and is considered by some to be exercise, and by others to be a type of alternative medicine or meditative practice. From a philosophical perspective Qigong is believed to help develop human potential, allow access to higher realms of awareness, and awaken one's 'true nature'.

Quantum Physics - The study of the behaviour of matter and energy at the molecular, atomic, nuclear, and even smaller microscopic levels. In the early 20th century, it was discovered that the laws that govern macroscopic objects do not function the same in such small realms. In the realm of quantum physics, observing something actually influences the physical processes taking place. Light waves act like particles and particles act like waves (called wave particle duality). Matter can go from one spot to another without moving through the intervening space (called quantum tunnelling). Information moves instantly across vast distances. In fact, in quantum mechanics we discover that the entire universe is actually a series of probabilities.

R.E.M. (raphid eye movement) - REM sleep typically occupies 20–25% of total sleep, about 90–120 minutes of a night's sleep. REM sleep is considered the deepest stage of sleep, and normally occurs close to morning. During a night of sleep, one usually experiences about four or five periods of REM sleep; they are quite short at the beginning of the night and longer toward the end. Many animals and some people tend to wake, or experience a period of very light sleep, for a short time immediately after a bout of REM. The relative amount of REM sleep varies considerably with age. A newborn baby spends more than 80% of total sleep time in REM. During REM, the activity of the brain's neurons is quite similar to that during waking hours; for this reason, the REM-sleep stage may be called paradoxical sleep.

Rosicrucians - Studies or membership within a philosophical secret society said to have been founded in late medieval Germany by Christian Rosenkreuz. It holds a doctrine or theology "built on esoteric truths of the ancient past", which, "concealed from the average man, provide insight into nature, the physical universe and the spiritual realm." Rosicrucianism is symbolized by the Rosy Cross. In the early 17th century, the manifestos caused excitement throughout Europe by declaring the existence of a secret brotherhood of alchemists and sages who were preparing to transform the arts, sciences, religion, and political and intellectual landscape of Europe. Wars of politics and religion ravaged the continent. The works were re-issued several times and followed by numerous pamphlets, favorable and otherwise. Between 1614 and 1620, about 400 manuscripts and books were published which discussed the Rosicrucian documents.

Samadhi - Described as a non-dualistic state of consciousness in which the consciousness of the experiencing subject becomes one with the experienced object, and in which the mind becomes still, one-pointed or concentrated while the person remains conscious. In Buddhism, it can also refer to an abiding in which mind becomes very still but does not merge with the object of attention, and is thus able to observe and gain insight into the changing flow of experience. In Hinduism, samādhi can also refer to videha mukti or the complete absorption of the individual consciousness in the self at the time of death, usually referred to as mahasamādhi.

Sanskrit - Classical Sanskrit is the standard register as laid out in the grammar of Pāṇini, 4th century BCE and it has significantly influenced most modern languages of the Indian subcontinent, particularly in India, Pakistan, Sri Lanka and Nepal. The pre-Classical form of Sanskrit is known as Vedic Sanskrit, with the language of the Rigveda being the oldest and most archaic stage preserved, its oldest core dating back to as early as 1500 BCE. This qualifies Rigvedic Sanskrit as one of the oldest attestations of any Indo-Iranian language, and one of the earliest attested members of the Indo-European language family.

Siddha - A Siddham in Tamil(an Indian sub-continent dialect) means *'one who is accomplished'* and refers to perfected masters who, according to Hindu belief, have transcended the ahamkara (ego or I-maker), have subdued their minds to be subservient to their Awareness, and have transformed their bodies (composed mainly of dense Rajo-tama gunas) into a different kind of body dominated by sattva. This is usually accomplished only by persistent meditation. Siddhas are the liberated souls. They have completely ended the cycle of birth and death. They have reached the ultimate state of salvation. They do not have any karmas and they do not collect any new karmas. This state of true freedom is called Moksha. They are formless and have no passions and therefore are free from all temptations. A siddha has also been defined to refer to one who has attained a siddhi.

Siddhi - The siddhis as paranormal abilities are considered emergent abilities of an individual that is on the path to siddhahood, and do not define a siddha, who is established in the Pranav or Aum – the spiritual substrate of creation. The siddhi in its pure form means "the attainment of flawless identity with Reality (Brahman); perfection of Spirit." In the Hindu philosophy of Kashmir Shaivism (Hindu tantra), siddha also refers to a Siddha Guru who can by way of Shaktipat initiate disciples into Yoga.

Shaman - Shamans claim to gain knowledge and the power to heal in the spiritual world or dimension. Most shamans have dreams or visions that convey certain messages. Shamans may claim to have or have acquired many spirit guides, who they believe guide and direct them in their travels in the spirit world. These spirit guides are always thought to be present within the shaman, although others are said to encounter them only when the shaman is in a trance. The spirit guide energizes the shamans, enabling them to enter the spiritual dimension. Shamans claim to heal within the spiritual dimension by returning lost parts of the human soul from wherever they have gone. Shamans also claim to cleanse excess negative energies, which are said to confuse or pollute the soul.

Shamans act as mediators in their cultures. Shamans claim to communicate with the spirits on behalf of the community, including the spirits of the deceased. Shamans believe they can communicate with both living and dead to alleviate unrest, unsettled issues, and to deliver gifts to the spirits.

Smudging - In some First Nations and Native American ceremonies, certain herbs are traditionally used to purify or bless people and places. For instance, some cultures use the smoke of burning red cedar as part of their particular purification and healing ceremonies. Sometimes this is done in hospitals to cleanse and repel evil influence.

Soul or **Soul Group** - The incorporeal and immortal essence of a person, living thing, or object. Souls which are immortal and capable of union with the divine belong only to human beings. 12 Souls are grouped together in a Soul Group which is governed by an Over Soul. 12 Soul Groups are governed by a Monad.

Solar Gazing - Hira Ratan Manek (HRM), among others, have proven eating any food. The method is used for curing all kinds of psychosomatic, mental and physical illnesses as well as increasing memory power and mental strength by using sunlight. One can get rid of any kind of psychological problems, and develop confidence to face any problem in life and can overcome any kind of fear including that of death within 3 months after starting to practice this method. As a result, one will be free from mental disturbances and fear, which will result in a perfect balance of mind.

If one continues to apply the proper sun gazing practice for 6 months, they will be free from physical illnesses. Furthermore, after 9 months, one can eventually win a victory over hunger, which disappears by itself thereafter. This is a straight-forward yet effective method based on solar energy, which enables one to harmonize and recharge the body with life energy and also invoke the unlimited powers of the mind very easily. Additionally, it allows one to easily liberate from threefold sufferings of humanity such as mental illnesses, physical illnesses and spiritual ignorance.

Spirit Guides - A term used by the Western tradition of Spiritualist Churches, mediums, and psychics to describe an entity that remains a disincarnate spirit in order to act as a guide or protector to a living incarnated human being. Traditionally, within the spiritualist churches, spirit guides were often stereotyped ethnically, with Native Americans, Chinese or Egyptians being popular for their perceived ancient wisdom.

Other popular types of guides were saints or other enlightened individuals. The term can also refer to totems, angels, guardian angels or nature spirits.

Spirit guides are not always of human descent. Some spirit guides live as energy, in the cosmic realm, or as light beings, which are very high level spirit guides. Some spirit guides are persons who have lived many former lifetimes, paid their karmic debts, and advanced beyond a need to reincarnate. Many devotees believe that spirit guides are chosen on "the other side" by human beings who are about to incarnate and wish assistance.

Tai Chi - A type of internal Chinese martial art practiced for both its defense training and its health benefits. It is also typically practiced for a variety of other personal reasons: its hard and soft martial art technique, demonstration competitions, and longevity. As a result, a multitude of training forms exist, both traditional and modern, which correspond to those aims. Some of Tai Chi Chuan's training forms are especially known for being practiced at what most people categorize as slow movement.

Tantra or **tantric** - Defined primarily as a technique-rich style of spiritual practice, Tantra has no single coherent doctrine; rather, it developed different teachings in connection with the different religions that adopted the Tantric method. These teachings tended to support and validate the practices of Tantra, which in their classical form are more oriented to the married householder than the monastic or solitary renunciant, and thus exhibited what may be called a world-embracing rather than a world-denying character. Thus Tantra, especially in its nondual forms, rejected the renunciant values of Patañjalian yoga, offering instead a vision of the whole of reality as the self-expression of a single, free and blissful Divine Consciousness under whatever name, whether Śiva or Buddha-nature.

Since the world was viewed as real, not illusory, this doctrine was a significant innovation over and against previous Indian philosophies, which tended to picture the Divine as absolutely transcendent and / or the world as illusion. The practical consequence of this view was that not only could householders aspire to spiritual liberation in the Tantric system, they were the type of practitioner that most Tantric manuals had in mind. Furthermore, since Tantra dissolved the dichotomy of spiritual versus mundane, practitioners could entail every aspect of their daily lives into their spiritual growth process, seeking to realize the transcendent in the immanent.

Tantric spiritual practices and rituals thus aim to bring about an inner realization of the truth that *"Nothing exists that is not Divine"* (nāśivaṃ vidyate kvacit), bringing freedom from ignorance and from the cycle of suffering (saṃsāra) in the process. In fact, tantric visualizations are said to bring the meditator to the core of his humanity and oneness with transcendence. Tantric meditations do not serve the function of training or practicing extra beliefs or unnatural ways. On the contrary, the transcendence that is reached by such meditative work does not construct anything in the mind of the practitioner, but actually de-constructs all preconceived notions of the human condition. The barriers that constrict thinking to limitation, namely, cultural and linguistic frameworks are completely removed. This allows the person to experience total liberation and then unity with ultimate truth or reality.

Thymus gland - The thymus is a specialized organ of the immune system. The thymus *"educates"* T-lymphocytes (T cells), which are critical cells of the adaptive immune system. Each T cell attacks a foreign substance which it identifies with its receptor. T cells have receptors which are generated by randomly shuffling gene segments. Each T cell attacks a different antigen. T cells that attack the body's own proteins are eliminated in the thymus. Thymic epithelial cells express major proteins from elsewhere in the body, and T cells that respond to those proteins are eliminated through programmed cell death (apoptosis). The thymus is composed of two identical lobes and is located in front of the heart and behind the sternum.

Thalamus Gland - (from Greek "chamber") It is a large mass of gray matter located in the dorsal part of the diencephalon (a division of the forebrain). Nerve fibers project out of the thalamus to the cerebral cortex in all directions, allowing hub-like exchanges of information. It has several functions, such as relaying of sensory signals, including motor signals to the cerebral cortex, and the regulation of consciousness, sleep, and alertness.

Tao - Chinese word meaning *'way'*, *'path'*, *'route'*, or sometimes more loosely, *'doctrine'* or *'principle'*. Within the context of traditional Chinese philosophy and religion, Tao is a metaphysical concept originating with Laozi that gave rise to a religion (Wade–Giles, Tao Chiao; Pinyin, Daojiao) and philosophy (Wade–Giles, Tao chia; Pinyin, Daojia) referred to in English with the single term Taoism. The concept of Tao was later adopted in Confucianism, Chán and Zen Buddhism and more broadly throughout East Asian philosophy and religion in general. Within these contexts Tao signifies the primordial essence or fundamental nature of the universe. In the foundational text of Taoism, the Tao Te Ching, Laozi explains that Tao is not a *'name'* for a *'thing'* but the underlying natural order of the universe whose ultimate essence is difficult to circumscribe. Tao is thus *'eternally nameless'* (Dao De Jing-32. Laozi) and to be distinguished from the countless 'named' things which are considered to be its manifestations.

Violet Flame - The Violet Flame is a Divine gift and tool for everyone, given to us by Ascended Master Saint Germain. It is a sacred fire that exists on the Higher Dimensions. People with the gift of inter-dimensional sight have seen it. Cameras have captured it when it was not visible to the person taking the photo. The Violet Flame is REAL and I invite you to use it to your great advantage. The Violet Flame is Spiritual Alchemy in action. Just as

Alchemy is said to turn Lead into Gold, the ultimate purpose of the Violet Flame is to turn the Human into the Divine Human. Its action is to TRANSMUTE denser feelings, actions, deeds, karma, etc., into a higher vibrational frequency, which helps prepare us for our Ascension

Vipassana-In the Buddhist tradition means insight into the true nature of reality. A regular practitioner of Vipassana, is known as a Vipassi. Vipassana is one of the world's most ancient techniques of meditation, which was introduced by Gautama Buddha. It is a practice of self-transformation through self-observation and introspection to the extent that sitting with a steadfast mind becomes an active experience of change and impermanence. In the west, Vipassanā meditation is often referred to simply as *"insight meditation"*.

Wheel of Life - The bhavacakra (Sanskrit; Pali: bhavacakka; Tibetan: srid pa'i 'khor lo) is a symbolic representation of samsara (or cyclic existence) found on the outside walls of Tibetan Buddhist temples and monasteries in the Indo-Tibetan region. In the Mahayana Buddhist tradition, it is believed that the drawing was designed by the Buddha himself in order to help ordinary people understand the Buddhist teachings. The bhavacakra is popularly referred to as the wheel of life. This term is also translated as wheel of cyclic existence or wheel of becoming.

Yantra - Is the Sanskrit word for "instrument" or "machine". Much like the word "instrument" itself, it can stand for symbols, processes, automata, machinery or anything that has structure and organization, depending on context. One usage popular in the west is as symbols or geometric figures. Traditionally such symbols are used in Eastern mysticism to balance the mind or focus it on spiritual concepts. The act of wearing, depicting, enacting and/or concentrating on a yantra is held to have spiritual, astrological or magical benefits in the Tantric traditions of the Indian religions.

Experience
the Special Edition
Journey to the
Akashic Records

• 390 pages 2 Glossaries
• Multiple meditation and energy techniques
• Multiple Akashic Guided Journeys
• Never Before Shared Information concerning the streaming of the Akashic Records and your Soul's connection to it!
• Many new Perspectives.

Available at www.billfoss.net
or Amazon

SPECIAL EDITION

JOURNEY TO THE AKASHIC RECORDS

A HANDBOOK & FIELD GUIDE
TO THE LIBRARY OF SOULS
AND OPENING YOUR BOOK OF LIFE

WITH

BILL FOSS

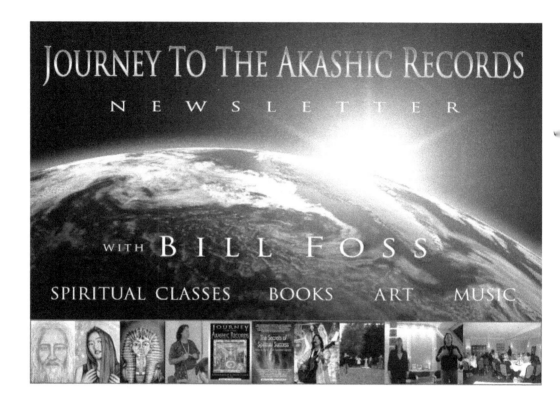

Check out the monthly newsletter for:
- Meditation insights and tips
- Upcoming workshop locations
- Personal individual sessions
- CD's and Downloads
- New Art & More!

www.billfoss.net

The "Journey to the Akashic Records" Study Set!
For Home Study and the Workshops Into the Akashic
Records!
Available at billfoss.net

320

The "Journey to the Akasha" Guided Journey Set
Study, Practice, and Learn New Ways of Opening
Into the Akashic Records - 4 CD's
Available from www.billfoss.net or Amazon

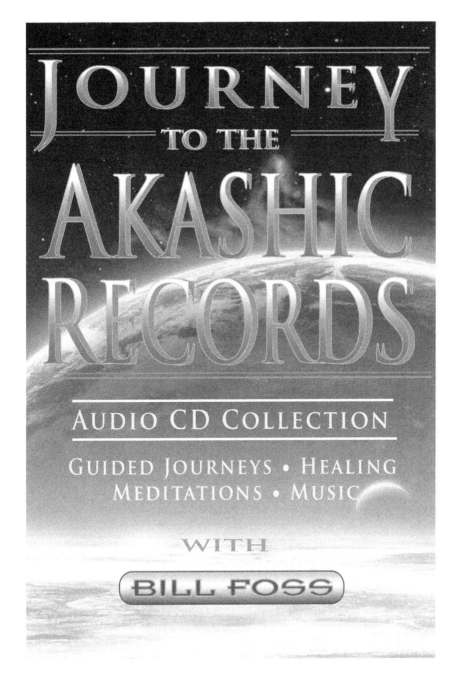

The "Journey to the Akasha" Workbook!
Study, Practice, and Learn New Ways of Opening
Into the Akashic Records!
Available from www.billfoss.net or Amazon

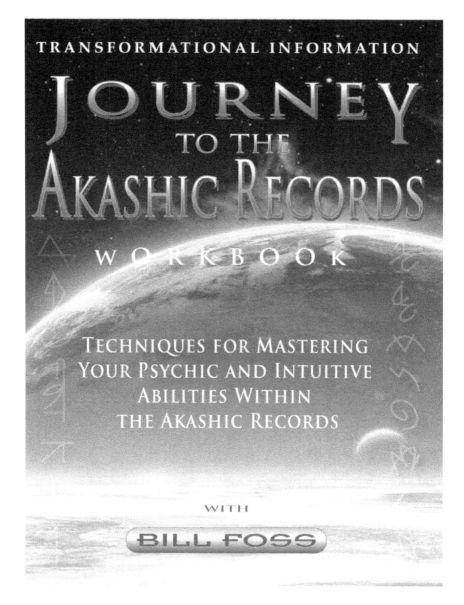

The "Journey to the Akasha" Workbook, Is the study companion workbook for all the exercises at the workshops, presentations and classes. This workbook will help you open and expand your abilities while giving you insight to strengthen your practice or working with your intuitive and healing abilities. Size 8.5" x 11" 165 Pages

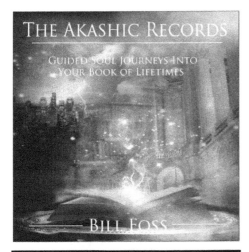

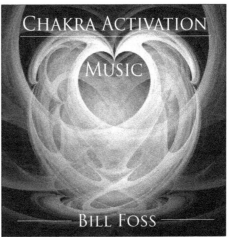

**Meditation
& Music
CDs &
Downloads**

billfoss.net

"Across The Universe through All Space and Time, the Creator has an Essence which flows through all things. Ever Present, Ever Watchful, Ever Compassionate. Waiting for the Moment when we come to recognize The Presence. Transforming our lives, others and the rest of our world into the Masterpiece as described by the Masters and indicated in all of the Sacred Texts and Ancient Teachings. May that Moment find You Now!"

The Secrets of Spiritual Success
Keys to the Art of an Abundant Lifestyle

Know Thyself · Service & Selflessness · Realization & Enlightenment
Power & Radiance · Opening the Senses · The Scene & the Unseen
Guidance & Counsel · Introspection & the External · Witness & Truth
Meditation & Prayer · Finding Love & Joy · Action & Awareness
Imagination & Intuition · Creativity & Visualization
Accessing the Soul, God & Self · Gratitude
Conceive, Believe & Receive

by BILL FOSS

The Secrets of Spiritual Success is a clear and concise road map providing an overview of understanding of 1000's of years of spiritual teachings, inquiries, and understandings. This book will help you to connect the dots more quickly in life, while adding to your studies already in motion or providing a great primer source to get started from. Whether you are a mystical student from beyond or you are new to expanded views and just looking for answers, this book was created to enliven and enrich your search, practices and studies. This book will turn on the lights for you and keep them on." Size 6" x 9" 237 Pages

Book • Workbook • Journal
Complete Study Set - Order at www.billfoss.net or Amazon

"The Keys of Spiritual Success" Workbook, companion to "The Secrets of Spiritual Success" is a collection of creative visualization and healing techniques, energy exercises, meditations, prayers. Exercises and insights to jump start your journey into your own long awaited or continued self inquiry and realization. Use this Workbook to Journal your subtle and not so subtle experiences as you open to greater understandings, fresh ideas, and new ways of being!" Size 8.5" x 11" 165 Pages

"The "Book Of Dreams" Journal is your gateway into creativity. This is your Journal, your space to create. What will you write, sketch, plan, or invent? Take the opportunity to go within and explore the vast regions, depths, and banks of Divine Creative Potential existing within you, all around you, throughout time, space & beyond. This is your chance to write down, plan and draw out your dream and make it a reality. Use this book as you will to expand your vision. It all starts here, and it starts with you so let's begin. Size 8.5" x 11" 165 Pages

Art Prints of the Spiritual Masters
Originals and Special Orders Available
at www.billfossworld.com

Notes:

Notes:

Notes:

CPSIA information can be obtained
at www.ICGtesting.com
Printed in the USA
LVHW010535030420
652112LV00005B/836